*Arthur Gerald*

# TALLY-HO!

## YANKEE IN A SPITFIRE

Copyright © 1942
Arthur Gerald Donahue

*TALLY-HO!*
*YANKEE IN A SPITFIRE*

*(1942)*

# CONTENTS

CHAPTER ONE - A FARM BOY GOES ABROAD..................................................9

CHAPTER TWO - APPRENTICESHIP IN WAR!.................................................15

CHAPTER THREE - TALLY HO!..........................................................................25

CHAPTER FOUR - VICTORY — AND ITS PRICE............................................34

CHAPTER FIVE - DEFEAT...................................................................................42

CHAPTER SIX - RECOVERY................................................................................49

CHAPTER SEVEN - BACK TO WORK................................................................53

CHAPTER EIGHT - IMPATIENCE.......................................................................58

CHAPTER NINE - BACK TO THE FRONT — TALLY-HO AGAIN................64

CHAPTER TEN - HUN-CHASING.......................................................................71

CHAPTER ELEVEN - A DAY AT WAR................................................................80

CHAPTER TWELVE - WE STAGE A COMEBACK...........................................93

CHAPTER THIRTEEN - INTERLUDE.................................................................99

CHAPTER FOURTEEN - THE WATCH OVER THE CHANNEL...................103

# TALLY-HO!
## YANKEE IN A SPITFIRE

To a certain very gallant officer and aviator,
without whose kindnesses this would probably
not have been written, but whom I must leave
unnamed until brighter days

# CHAPTER ONE

# A FARM BOY GOES ABROAD

I'M AFRAID that if this story is to be judged by the standards of the thousands of air stories that have been available to the American public in magazines the last few years, it will be classed as a failure. It is not very bloodcurdling, with fewer people taking part in the entire story than meet death in the first three pages of most air stories.

The hero is not tall and muscular and steely-eyed, with grim, wind-bitten, hawklike features; and his accomplishments in the story are few. Worse yet, he's anything but fearless; he scares as easily as you do, perhaps more easily, and in the whole story he never does anything particularly heroic. Worst of all is his identity, because actually he's only me.

But this story is true, and I hope that some of you may consider its shortcomings compensated for by the fact that the characters in this story really exist — or existed; that the occurrences in this story, though less spectacular, really occurred; and that the characters who meet death in it really did meet death, in the savage and desperate struggle that is being fought for the safety of the world, including you.

The most that can be said for myself is that I tried and tried hard, and fought hard, as I hope to be still trying and fighting when you read this; and I have probably accomplished as much against the enemy as the average of those who were in action at the same times as I. And I did have the privilege of being numbered among the few score pilots who met the first German mass onslaughts in the Air Blitzkrieg against England. Of these facts I shall always be proud, even if I fail to add more to them.

And in this tale of an ordinary American from a Midwest farm coming to a warring country, joining its fighting forces, mingling with its fighting men, and finally fighting and falling and fighting again, I hope that I can tell you enough of "what it's like" to keep your interest. If I fail it will be my fault as a writer, for I'm sure that what I've seen and experienced will interest average Americans if I describe it right. I'm an ordinary American myself, and it has been tremendously interesting to me!

I was born and raised on a farm at St. Charles, Minnesota, and at the age of eighteen I went into commercial flying. During the years of the depression this wasn't always too lucrative, and at various times I worked as garage mechanic, construction worker, and truck driver, in addition to working on my father's farm quite often. Always, however, I tried to work at some place where I could also keep my hand in flying part of the time — barnstorming, instructing, and the like, and working as aircraft mechanic. For the most part of the year and a half before I went to war I was engaged as an instructor at the International Flying School at Laredo, Texas.

As I remember, when I started flying there were about a hundred and twenty licensed pilots in Minnesota; and if you had lined us all up at that time and ranked us according to our possibilities of ever flying in a war, I'd have been in about the one hundred nineteenth place. The only one less likely than myself would have been my good friend Shorty Deponti of Minneapolis. Shorty would never fly in a war for two very good reasons: first, there wasn't enough money in it; and second, there wasn't enough money in it. My flying instructor, Max Conrad of Winona, would be more easily moved because he'd get higher pay out of allowances for his five daughters. I didn't have any of the qualifications of a soldier. I was neither big nor very strong; I was quite mild-tempered and absolutely afraid to fight, and I was more cautious in my flying than the average pilot then. Yet I believe I am the only one of them all to have gone to war. Tom Hennessy, whom I'd have ranked in those days as the most likely prospect, is now married and settled down sensibly on an airline.

When the war started I should have liked to volunteer at once for England. I felt that this was America's war as much as England's and France's, because America was part of the world, which Hitler and his minions were so plainly out to conquer. Consideration for my folks, whom I didn't want to saddle with a lot of worries, held me back. As the next best thing, I applied for a commission in the United States Army Air Corps Reserve, so that I could learn something about military flying anyway. This looked easy on paper, but I found myself frustrated for months by delays that were mostly hard to understand.

I paid a visit home in mid-June of 1940, and was cultivating corn on my dad's farm at the time of the collapse of France and the evacuation of Dunkirk. I had heard that American pilots were being hired for noncombatant jobs with the Royal Air Force, so when I left home I went to Canada to investigate. I was promptly hired, and about ten days later I boarded a boat for England.

It was a big passenger liner and should have been gayly painted and lighted, with flags flying and decks lined with tourists as it sailed — at least that's the way they were in all the pictures I'd seen. But instead it was painted in dull drab colors and there were only a handful of passengers. Nevertheless it was my first ocean trip, and I was plenty thrilled. Orders were posted about that we must keep our portholes closed at night and not show any lights on deck; and I realized that whether I fought or not I was in part of the war now.

I boarded the ship in late afternoon, and after I was settled and had had my supper I went out on deck. We were sailing down the St. Lawrence River and it was nearly dark. Not a light showed on the ship. At the stern I saw some men on a platform above the main deck swinging what looked like the boom of a big crane out so it hung over the water, and I wondered what they intended to lift with a crane out there. Then my eyes became accustomed to the darkness and I saw that it wasn't a crane at all, but a big cannon being prepared for use — more evidence of war! Remember, I was just an ordinary American, to whom war and battles and actual shooting at human targets were unreal things that only occurred in newspapers or movies or books. This was real, and it wasn't in a newspaper or movie or book, and I just stood there awhile gauping at it!

I enjoyed every moment of the trip across. I had a whole cabin to myself, and the excellence of the service and food gave me a feeling of luxury. Here on the smooth Atlantic life was so peaceful and relaxed that it was difficult to remember, except when I looked at the grim cannon at the stern of the ship, that within a few days I should be among a people fighting for existence, with their backs to the wall.

The prettiest sight of the trip was furnished by a number of icebergs one afternoon — something I didn't expect to see in July. The sun was shining brightly, making them appear crystal-white and gleaming. We were nearly always within sight of half a dozen, for several hours, and we sailed quite close to some. One which passed close had apparently shifted its position in the water, and a wide ring of blue marking its old water line was visible. It contrasted beautifully with the white of the rest of the iceberg, cutting across it diagonally. The blue band, I suppose, was clear pure ice, while the rest of the berg was ice and snow, very white. It was about a mile away and was at least one hundred fifty feet high. It was one of the most beautiful and striking pieces of scenery nature ever produced.

We arrived in an English port on a dreary, foggy Sunday morning after a final twenty-four hours of constant zigzagging by our ship to upset the aim of any lurking enemy submarines. The ship stood in midstream for hours while we passengers leaned on the deck railings and dodged the sea gulls that flapped overhead, squawking and bombing indiscriminately.

We left the ship in late afternoon and an R.A.F. officer took me in tow and escorted me from the dock to a green and tan camouflaged automobile which was parked near by. Instead of a license plate on the front of the car there was a plate with three big letters: "R.A.F."

My baggage having been loaded on, we set out for the railway station, and I got my first look at an English city. I had never realized that English cities were so different from American cities, with their winding irregular streets and their closely packed stone houses and business buildings of wholly different architecture from ours. Traffic is left-hand in England, and it seemed impossible for so many cars to be driving on the wrong side of the street with no accidents! I expected we'd crack up every minute. We didn't, though, and at the railway station the officer got me a ticket for London.

I found that my train didn't leave until midnight, so I set out to find a restaurant and eat supper. On the ship each passenger had received a gas mask in a little cardboard carrying case, and I now carried mine. However, after walking about a block I realized that it looked out of place. No one else carried any, and people were staring at mine. I went back to the station and put it away in my suitcase!

Then I sallied forth again and found a restaurant; but I still didn't get any supper. I understood but little of the menu on the wall and nothing of the prices, which were in English money of course, with its set of signs absolutely foreign to any American. Furthermore I realized that I didn't have any idea of how you ordered a meal here, and I just didn't have the nerve to try to bluff it. Retreating to the station once more, I got some chocolate bars from an automatic vender.

After a time an English girl came in whom I had met on the boat, and I found that she was waiting for the same train. At my suggestion we went out together for supper, and by that time it was dark.

And I mean dark. Not a street light showed, not a window or doorway gave a crack of light. It was my first experience in a black-out, of course. The few cars and busses on the street crawled along at five miles an hour, with nothing but dim little parking lights to see by. Many of the people walking had lighted cigarettes, and it helped them to keep from running into each other. That was once I wished that I was a smoker.

There was a sense of freedom about it, though, for we could walk in the middle of the street, as many did, because the cars moved so slowly that we didn't have to worry about being run down. We just stepped out of their way! There were a few very dim stop and go lights, and here and there dim blue lights marking the entrances to air-raid shelters. These and the little lights of cars, the glowing cigarette tips, and an occasional dimmed flashlight were the only breaks in the darkness. Posts, stairways, building corners, and similar objects were all painted white so that people wouldn't walk into them.

That was a cloudy night. On clear nights it isn't so bad and the traffic moves faster, particularly if there is moonlight too. Houses and buildings, of course, have their windows and doorways curtained so that the lights can be used inside; and until I got used to it I always had a sensation of bewilderment when I stepped out of a brightly lighted restaurant or other building, absently expecting to be in a brightly lighted street, and then found nothing outside but total darkness.

The passenger car in which we rode to London was divided into little carriagelike compartments, each having room for four passengers riding forward and four facing backward. The lights in our compartment were very dim and shielded so they only lit up a little section of the middle of it, and even then we had to have curtains drawn all around. We rode "First Class." "Third Class" coaches are less comfortable, but are cheaper; there isn't any second class. I marveled at the speed the train made through the blacked-out country. The locomotive used only the faintest headlights or none at all, and the engineers must have had cats' eyes to do it.

I'm still glad it was a beautiful fresh morning when we walked out of the station at the end of the journey, for my first glimpse of the world's greatest city.

I'll always try to keep my first impression of London, for it will never be like that again. The streets, houses, buildings, trees, and parks were all at their best in the bright sunlight. Far overhead the silvery barrage balloons hung silent and motionless, like sentinels. The raids hadn't begun then, nor the devastation. But every one knew they were coming; and London impressed me so much with its greatness and beauty as it stood that morning awaiting its trial, prepared and unafraid.

It's hard to give a specific reason why I became a combat pilot. Of course I'd always wanted to be one; and once I was in England the significance of the struggle seemed to carry me away. This was mid-July. France had fallen, and the invasion of England seemed imminent. Its success would open the whole world to a barbarian conquest. I had a growing admiration for the British people and a sincere desire to help them all I could. I couldn't help feeling that it would be fighting for my own country, too.

I felt drawn into the struggle like a moth to a candle. That's a pretty good comparison, too, for it developed that I was to get burned once and be drawn right back into it again!

Knowing that one of England's greatest problems was inferiority in numbers in the air, I felt it a duty as a follower of the civilized way of life to throw my lot in if they would take me. To fight side by side with these people against the enemies of civilization would be the greatest of all privileges. I had never done any military flying, but was confident of my ability to adapt myself.

Inquiries revealed that the way was wide open. I could be a fighter (pursuit) pilot if I wished, by first taking an advanced training course. Also I could probably get where the fighting was heaviest if I wished, because pilots as a rule were given preference in this regard. I shouldn't need to tell my folks I was fighting, because they wouldn't expect me to tell much about my work on account of censorship. The whole set-up had too much appeal for my resistance.

I knew I should be scared to death many times and should regret my decision often, for as I said before, I am not overendowed with courage; but I also knew that I'd never forgive myself if I rejected this opportunity. So in a fateful moment on the day after my arrival I held my pen poised while making one last reflection on what I was doing, and then signed on the dotted line. I thereby surrendered my independence for the duration of the war and became a proud member of the Royal Air Force. I also presumed that I was surrendering my citizenship, for I understood that the law was so interpreted at that time.

I was given a commission as pilot officer, which corresponds to the rank of second lieutenant in the Army; and was allowed two days' leave to buy a uniform. I was impressed with the swiftness and lack of red tape with which I was accepted. I had simply shown them that I had the goods and they had said in effect: "All right. We'll buy. Sign here, and you can start delivering." It was a refreshing contrast to my experiences in my own country.

My uniform was soon made up, and on the evening of the fourth day after arrival in England I walked down the streets of London a full-fledged officer of His Majesty's Royal Air Force. That is, I walked a little way. I was with an American boy working in London whom I'd met the day before, and who was going to show me about. We walked about a block and then met a couple of airmen in uniform ("airmen" is the term for all noncommissioned ranks in the R.A.F.). They of course saluted me as an officer; and I of course was obliged to return their salute. Then the terrible realization dawned on me — not having been inducted into the R.A.F. in the normal way, I hadn't learned how to salute!

It was do or die, though, and I "did" — in a terribly blundering fashion, it seemed to me; and I fancied them to be staring back at me, wondering what was wrong. There were plenty of soldiers and airmen on the streets, and by the time I'd walked a few more blocks and been saluted half a dozen times I had lost all interest in the sights.

I said to my companion: "This can't go on. Let's find a café or restaurant where we can stay inside until after dark."

He suggested a little place on Kingsway, where we could get American Coca-Cola, and I sighed thankfully as we entered this haven. There was a girl sitting at the table next to us, in the uniform of the Women's Auxiliary Air Force. This is the women's branch of the R.A.F. Its members work side by side with R.A.F. men at R.A.F. stations, doing work that they are capable of, and their status is exactly the same. They are usually called "Waffs" from the initials of their organization, W.A.A.F. I appealed to her, and she instructed me in the proper way of saluting. I suppose that was one of the few times in history when a member of the ranks instructed an officer on how to salute!

Fortified with this instruction and a little practice I felt safe in sallying forth again, and we went for a long walk about the interesting parts of the town, looking at some of the sights I had often read about — Buckingham Palace, St. James's Palace, the buildings of Parliament, the great clock "Big Ben," the home of Scotland Yard, Trafalgar Square, and many other places that were a big thrill to me. Even bigger were the thrills I got walking past Buckingham and St. James's Palaces when the guards there presented arms to me, and I began to realize what a weight of tradition I had taken on when I put on the King's uniform for my first time that evening.

One didn't have to walk far through London then to realize there was going to be no thought of declaring it an "open city," or of abandoning it except building by building and street by street if the barbarian Hun came; and I began to realize that the type of resistance that the Nazis would face here was very different from what confronted them in France.

London was a fortress. Anti-tank barriers and traps were located all about. Sandbag and concrete barricades and breastworks were erected everywhere, protected every building. Gun emplacements marred the beauty of the parks.

The Prime Minister had said, "We shall not falter." I got a feeling, realizing the implication of all these preparations, that history would prove him right.

# CHAPTER TWO

# APPRENTICESHIP IN WAR!

NEXT DAY I journeyed by train to the advanced training school to which I had been assigned. Traveling this time by day, I found the English landscape surprisingly like that of southern Wisconsin — rolling country, very green, with lots of small pastures and a great deal of woodland. The one big difference was that there were no red barns. Many of the barns in England, like other buildings, are of stone, and the rest all seem to be painted white or gray.

My school was one of many such that are known as "Operational Training Units." At these places newly trained pilots are given their final brushing up and actual experience in flying the latest fighter planes under the guidance of experienced fighter pilots who teach them the newest tactics. In addition, experienced pilots who have been doing other kinds of flying and want to become fighter pilots, as well as pilots from other air forces, receive the same training in order to learn British fighting tactics and the behavior of fighting planes. There were many Polish pilots and a few Belgians at this place undergoing training.

It was my first visit to a wartime airdrome, and I found it an impressive contrast to airports I was familiar with. In the United States everything possible is done to make an airport conspicuous and easy to locate — bright markings on hangars, buildings, etc., conspicuous runways, big arrows pointing toward the airport on the tops of buildings near by, and so on, for the convenience of visiting pilots.

The visiting pilots who come here are not welcome, and everything is done to hide the airdrome from them. Hangars, shops, offices, and even driveways and roads are camouflaged, as well as vehicles themselves. All are painted in crazy wavy combinations of dull greens, grays, browns, and black, so designed that at great altitudes the airdrome merges in with the countryside and can scarcely be seen.

Most impressive of all to me was the grim dull coloring of the airplanes themselves. They were painted dull green and brown in the wavy pattern, except the undersides, which were gray. Concession is made even in the national markings, which for British planes consist of a red bull's-eye surrounded by concentric white and blue rings. On the top side of the wings this is altered by omitting the white ring, because that is too conspicuous from above, so there is just a larger red bull's-eye and a wider blue ring around it. The Spitfire fighting planes have a peculiarly shaped wing, very wide and tapered in such a way that it resembles the wings of some moths. The round red and blue marking near each tip enhances this resemblance so much that the planes themselves look like giant moths from above.

The entire airdrome bristled with sandbags, trenches, dugouts, and machine-gun and anti-aircraft emplacements.

A building known as the "officers' mess" is provided for officers at airdromes and other military stations in England. This usually contains a dining room, bar, billiard room, and a large comfortable lounge. Here the officers spend most of their leisure time, and the officers' mess is a large part of their life. The building may or may not contain quarters for the officers as well. At this station it did not, and we roomed in other buildings. Each officer has the services of a "batman," or valet, who takes care of his room, makes his bed, presses his uniform, polishes his buttons, wakens him in the morning, and in general makes himself useful. This was all quite strange to me, and I went to bed pondering on the many strange things I must get used to in fighting the Huns.

Next morning I was assigned to a "flight" of several pilots who arrived for training at the same time I did, and I reported to my flight commander's office. While waiting to see him I read a notice on the wall advising students to take their training here seriously. I still remember the closing words: "... for in all probability this is the last training you will receive before being committed to combat with the enemy."

It gave me a little thrill. I was getting close to realities.

An instructor took me up in an American-built military plane, a North American, which is a type widely used for advanced training here, and I did a couple of landings for him. He seemed satisfied and assigned me to a single-seat advanced trainer of English make and gave me some practice work to do in it.

I had never flown anything that cruised faster than one hundred ten miles per hour before I left the States. This machine cruised at one hundred eighty; and I thought it more wonderful than anything I'd ever imagined. I practiced in it for a few days and then was told I might go on to flying Spitfires.

This was the very height of my hopes. Of all England's superb fighting planes, the Supermarine Spitfires are generally considered masters of them all and the world's deadliest fighters. The pilots assigned to fly them consider themselves the luckiest of pilots. They are single-seat low-wing monoplanes. The engines are twelve-cylinder Rolls Royce of about ten hundred fifty horsepower with an "emergency boost" giving them nearly fourteen hundred horsepower for actual combat. Each has eight machine gun, mounted in the wings. All the guns point forward and are fired by a single button on the top of the pilot's control stick. The Spitfires, together with the Hawker "Hurricanes" which are contemporary fighters also carrying eight guns, are often called "flying machine-gun nests." The cruising speed of a Spitfire is nearly three hundred miles per hour and the top speed nearly four hundred.

To myself, who had been instructing for the last year and a half in trainers of forty horsepower that cruised at sixty miles per hour, this was such a change that there just didn't seem to be any connection with my former flying. The first time I took a Spitfire up, I felt more like a passenger than a pilot. However, I began to get used to the speed after a few hours. I practiced acrobatics mainly at first, to get familiar with the behavior of the airplanes. In doing this I got my initiation to a new factor, which limits a pilot's ability to maneuver at high speeds. This factor is known as the "black-out" — no connection with the black-out of cities at night.

If you swing a pail of water over your head the water will stay in the pail even when it is upside down, because centrifugal force pushes it against the bottom of the pail. Similarly, if an airplane is turned or looped quickly the centrifugal force tends to push the blood in the pilot's body downward, toward the bottom of the plane and away from his head. In ordinary airplanes this doesn't matter because his heart keeps pumping the blood right back up to his head. But modern fighting (pursuit) planes are so fast that it is quite easy in a turn or loop for the centrifugal force to drain the blood from the pilot's head. When this happens his brain stops working. At three hundred miles per hour only a few degrees of change in direction per second is enough to cause a pilot to "black out." A pilot's physical strength in resisting black-out is what determines the rate at which he can turn at high speeds, but it is impossible for any pilot to turn very quickly at three hundred miles an hour or more.

Strangely, when one starts to black out in a turn or loop his eyes fail before his brain. My first experience in blacking out occurred the first time I tried to loop in a Spitfire. I was cruising along at about two hundred eighty and drew the control stick back about an inch, rather abruptly, to start my loop. Instantly the airplane surged upward in response, so hard that I was jammed down in the seat, feeling terribly heavy, feeling my cheeks sag downward and my mouth sag open from the centrifugal force on my lower jaw, and a misty, yellowish gray curtain closed off my vision! I eased the stick forward again to stop the change in direction and my sight came back instantly. I saw that I had raised the nose of the plane only a few degrees.

This loss of vision is the warning a pilot receives. If he continues to turn or loop that hard he will lose consciousness in a few seconds. In looping I found that I had to ease the nose up ever so slowly at first until the speed had dropped to around two hundred, after which I could pull the plane around quite fast without blacking out.

It's an uncanny thing. In combat you may be circling to get your guns to bear on the enemy. He is circling too, but you have almost caught up with him. He is just outside of your gunsights; and if you could only pull your plane around a few extra degrees, all at once, you would have him in your sights and be able to open fire. But you can't do that. You can turn just so fast and that is all, for if you turn any faster your vision fades and you can't see either him or your sights!

A pilot can increase his resistance to "black-out" by practice in doing lots of tight turns at high speed. He learns to contract the muscles of his abdomen and take deep breaths and hold them while he's turning, because that leaves less room for the blood to drain to down in his body. In this way physical strength often enters modern air fighting. The pilot who can resist black-out best is the one who can maneuver fastest at speeds much above 200.

Leaning forward also helps, because then one's head isn't as high above his heart, and so his heart can pump the blood up to his head easier. I have some very vivid recollections of moments in combat when trying to throw an enemy "off my tail" (in other words from directly behind me which is the best position to shoot from) when I was leaning forward as far as my straps would permit, taking big gasps of air and holding them, and tensing my body muscles in the desperation one feels when his life is at stake, trying to fight off that damnable misty curtain from my eyes while fairly hauling my plane around in the most sickening turns. It invariably worked, too, and when I "came up for air" after a few seconds and looked around I usually found that my enemy had lost his advantage and it was my turn to take the offensive.

There was an English boy named Peter, a big dark-haired husky fellow, who started this training course the same time I did. We took to each other as soon as we met, and became very close pals. He had been in the Navy at sixteen, and at twenty he was bronzed and hardened and looked and acted several years older. We practiced nearly all our flying together and with a squadron leader who was also taking the course.

We did a lot of "dog fighting" practice. We would take off together, Peter and I, and climb to ten or fifteen thousand feet. Then we would separate and fly in opposite directions a few seconds, so that we could turn around and fly back toward each other. Then when we'd meet we'd engage in vicious mock combats — turning, twisting, rolling, climbing, and diving to get into firing position on each other. When one of us succeeded in getting the other in his gunsights he pressed with his thumb on the guard over the firing button on his machine, sending salvo after salvo of imaginary bullets after his pal. This guard over the firing button was just a temporary affair, to keep the pilot from accidentally pressing the button itself when he didn't want to use the guns; and across it were painted in red letters the words "GUNS LOADED."

I became well acquainted with some of the Poles who were training here. They were a fine bunch of fellows. Most of them had fought the Hun over Poland and again in France. Now they were being prepared to fight with the Royal Air Force. They were cheerful, happy-go-lucky fellows — except when the subject of Nazis was brought up. Then you saw evidence of the terrible hatred for the dogs who had ravaged their homeland and their people.

On one occasion one of the English boys, joking, chided one of the Polish boys, saying that he was supposed to love his enemies. It didn't anger the other because he knew it was a jest; but he replied with a pitiful attempt to smile and keep his voice light, "Would you love your enemies when they kill your mother, and put your sister in a brothel for soldiers?"

I hope I never find myself in as perilous a position as that of a Nazi pilot being attacked by one of our Poles.

Days passed, and we began to develop a polish in our handling of the Spitfires. I had been at the training base about ten days when the papers carried the news that the State Department of the United States had announced that Americans fighting for Britain would not lose their citizenship. My friends congratulated me, and I felt pretty good. But I also felt proud that I hadn't waited to learn that before I volunteered.

In the lounge at the officers' mess I was often the center of conversations about the United States and the war. I was continually asked if I thought the United

States would join or at least give more help, and when. I answered their questions as well as I could, giving the American people's side as I had seen it but not necessarily taking that side. A mean of all such conversations would have run something like this:

"When's your country going to give us some help, America" ("America" is about the only nickname I have in England outside of the usual "Art").

"I don't know," I reply. "They've sent me, haven't they?"

"Yes, but we're never sure whether that was helping us or Germany. Seriously, though, what do they think about it — don't they realize this is a world menace we're fighting?"

"Yes," I admit, "most of them seem to realize it now. They seem pretty well agreed that if Hitler wins here it will only be a matter of time before their turn will come. But they'd rather have it that way, it seems, than to take any chances of having their boys fight on foreign soil."

"What? You mean they'd rather wait and fight in their own country?"

"I guess so," I admit again.

"Do you know what that means?"

"They should."

"Sounds as if they don't like their women and children," says one.

"Or their homes and cities," from another.

"Besides," I add, "they say, 'What did we get out of helping England in the last war?'"

"They got rid of their menace, didn't they? Where do they think they'd be if the Kaiser controlled England and France and Canada?"

"They forget that they ever had a menace then, and all they remember is that it cost them money."

"Do they think England got rich on it?"

"If you ask me, they don't think, very deeply."

I wasn't standing up for my countrymen in these conversations because I didn't sympathize with their attitude. I'd fight the battles which were America's as well as England's in the air, but I wouldn't fight America's battles in the officers' mess.

I had just come out of the officers' mess from dinner one noon when the local air-raid sirens sounded. It was the first air-raid warning I had ever heard.

It was a cloudy day, there being a high dark overcast that covered the sky. Lower down there were a lot of scattered thick clouds; and looking between these I could see, very high up, a long curving trail of smoke across the sky. I asked some of the boys who were watching what it was, and one of them said, "It must have been a Jerry made that. See, there's some Spitfires going up after him."

I could see several Spitfires above the clouds, and as I knew that my flight commander was up on a training flight with some of the boys I wondered if theirs were the Spitfires I could see. I had never seen a German airplane, and I strained my eyes trying to see this one, but couldn't.

Suddenly above the sound of the several engines roaring up there we heard a distant *r-r-rat-a-tat-tat*! The engines kept on droning as the machines scurried about, and now the Spitfires were so high we couldn't see them either. They all seemed to be working north of the airdrome.

All activity at the airdrome had of course stopped when the air-raid warning sounded, but no one was in shelter. Every one was outside trying to see the show. Now little black puffs of smoke began appearing here and there far up in the sky north of us, and a few seconds later we heard a succession of little noises like a feather duster being shaken outside a window — anti-aircraft shells exploding, I realized — the first time I had ever seen an attempt to take a human life. Then came a succession of heavy distant "booms" — bombs exploding, the others said.

Now the planes seemed to be getting closer overhead again. Another and longer *r-r-rat-a-tat-tat*! reached our ears and every one grew tense and breathless watching the sky. A long minute elapsed and then:

"There he is!" The voice of one of the overwrought boys who called out almost ended in a scream; and then we saw it too. First there was just an indistinct swirling in the bottom mists of one of the clouds, and then it came clear. It was an enormous strange-looking twin-engined airplane, and it was in a tailspin, nose down and gyrating 'round and 'round as it fell. It was the first time I had ever seen a big airplane in a tailspin, and I was spellbound.

"It's a Jerry all right!" said an awed voice.

A tiny figure parted from it, fell a way, and then the white canopy of a parachute blossomed above it. Then another and another came clear, and their parachutes blossomed out.

The great machine kept spinning down and down, seeming slow and majestic even in this, its death dive. As it got lower and lower I tried to realize that it wouldn't be recovering from the spin at the regulation 1500 feet minimum altitude, as exhibition or student planes that I watched always did. It wasn't going to pay any attention to the nearing ground. It was going to spin in! Almost unbelieving, I watched it make its last great corkscrewing revolution, just sweeping over the treetops of a near-by grove and disappearing behind them.

A moment later there was a heavy crash, and then every one was running in the direction of the grove and the victorious Spitfires were diving and zooming and rolling over the spot and some of them went to circling around the descending parachutes with their unhappy occupants, like Indians doing a dance around trussed-up captives. The Polish boys who were watching with us were very angry because none of the Spitfire pilots shot the Nazis in their parachutes — Nazi pilots had machine-gunned many Polish pilots in their parachutes in the Polish campaign!

We soon learned the whole story. The machine was a Junkers 88 bomber that had come to raid a near-by village. When the Spitfires took chase the pilot tried to get away, jettisoning his bombs in open country, but one of the Spitfires caught him anyway. It was the plane piloted by our flight commander; with his second burst of machine-gun fire he had dislodged one engine from the bomber so that it fell completely out of the airplane! The German pilot was then unable to control his unbalanced airplane and it went into the fatal tailspin. One other member of the crew bailed out in addition to the three we saw, but he wasn't as fortunate. They found his body in a wood. The rip-cord by which he could have opened his parachute was severed by a bullet.

***

Every day we wondered when the promised German invasion would start. This was the last of July and Hitler had promised to take over London by August 15th. Peter and I hoped the invasion wouldn't start until we finished our training. The mass air raids had not yet begun on England, but there was a great deal of air fighting over the English Channel.

We had made our requests to be posted to a squadron near the Channel — the same squadron for both of us if possible. Those were the squadrons getting the action now, and if the invasion were launched it seemed likely that the Channel would be the hottest place then, too. We were spoiling for all the action we could get.

Peter and I reported as usual in our flight commander's office on the morning of the day before our training was scheduled to end.

"What shall we do this morning, sir?" I asked, meaning what flying should we do.

He looked at us a little oddly and then said: "Nothing. You boys have been a little ahead of your schedule, and you've covered everything I can give you. The rest you'll have to learn — other ways!"

We knew what he meant by that. Our next instruction would be from our enemies!

"You boys can take the day off," he added.

We saluted and went out. When we were outside, we turned to each other and shook hands, grinning. Peter said, "Congratulations, war pilot!" We had arrived.

That afternoon we were informed, to our delight, that we had been posted to one of the squadrons close to the English Channel. We asked how close it was to the Channel and were told, "From your advance base you can see the French coast on a clear day!"

We were given railway warrants and told to leave the next afternoon. I spent most of the rest of the day studying pictures of German fighting and bombing planes.

Next morning we packed. In the afternoon a large lorry left the airport for the railway station carrying a precious cargo. More than a score of newly trained fighter pilots rode in it, all bound for various squadrons. Over half were Poles and Belgians, eager for vengeance; and most of them were to exact their vengeance from the Nazis soon.

We all took a train to London, where we separated on various lines for our destinations. There was plenty of handshaking and good-byes.

"Take care of yourself, and watch your tail, Pal!"

"Thanks, old man, same to you! Hope you get a hundred of them!"

Many well-wishes such as these, and then Peter and I were alone waiting for the train that would take us on a branch line to our squadron's home base, an airdrome near London.

Sitting and walking about in the gathering darkness, waiting for our train, we got to talking about America. It was Peter's ambition to go to America after the war, and to stay there if he could find a job with a future in it. I told him I thought it would be swell if we could go back to the States together after this was over, that I was sure he could find a job and get ahead. He said: "Let's plan on that. If we both come through this war in one piece I'll go back with you."

I thought of what a swell pal he'd be to have over in America, and was glad of the plan.

We arrived at our airdrome late in the evening, and were fixed up with rooms in the officers' mess and told to report to our squadron leader in the morning. We met some of our new mates, who hadn't gone to bed yet. Conversation was all about the news they had just received from one of the oldest members of the squadron. He had been missing since a battle over the Channel some time back, and had been counted as dead. Now they had received word that he was alive, a prisoner of war in a German hospital. They were jubilant over the news.

An elderly, thin-featured, dark-haired man in the uniform of a pilot officer introduced himself to us.

"My name's F——," he said, speaking slowly and with a solemn mien that was contradicted by a twinkle in his eye, "but every one calls me 'Number One.' You see, I am Number One stooge of your squadron. You know stooges are people who don't fly, don't you?

"There are three of us officer stooges in the squadron. We're really very nice people, too. I hardly count myself. I'm just the Intelligence officer, sort of a father-confessor to whom you are supposed to tell all the blows you've struck at your fellowmen, the Huns, each time after you come back from shooting holes in them. You'll meet the other stooges in the morning. 'Number Two' is the squadron's chief mechanic, and 'Number Three' is the adjutant."

We liked the man at once, and from the twinkle in his eye and the dry humor with which he spoke about himself and the rest we suspected that our squadron must be a good-natured bunch.

We were right. From commanding officer right down to the lowest ranks, they were all a cheerful, easy-natured, hard-working, happy-go-lucky group, an ideal bunch to work with or fight with or have fun with.

And as time went on I was to learn that the same was true of nearly all the boys and men in the R.A.F. — good-natured, fun-loving, informal chaps, laughing in the face of tragedy because it did no good to cry, and fighting because their country is forced to, not because it's their trade or because they want to. No professional soldiers, most of these: they are your brother who was working in a drugstore to earn money to go to college and study to be a lawyer, until his country had to rise to call a halt to world gangsterism; and young Joe who was doing well in the insurance office downtown; your neighbor's boy who had just graduated from high school and had his head full of changing ideas, all involving a secure future; the Smith boy who had just gotten married and settled down on his father's farm — his father is running the farm again now, after having planned to retire; and young Ray King, the spoiled, spendthrift, ne'er-do-well son of the local banker, who every one had prophesied would come to no good, chastised and sobered now by his consecration to a high cause.

Certainly no "international bankers," these lads, in whose plans war had had no part — nor in the plans of their parents either. Their parents, too, are ordinary people, who had approved their government's course in giving beaten Germany a chance to rise again so that her people could live happily and normally, until an insane, hate-crazed spellbinder had wrested control of the nation and turned it into a great war machine and started it on a march of world conquest and murder.

Then and only then, completely educated on both sides of the question by a free press, and by a free radio from which they could listen daily to thousands of words of Nazi propaganda in the English language, these ordinary people had risen and demanded that their government call a halt and make a stand now, because they could see that there was no other way out. And so these boys had abandoned all their cherished plans and gone into training to learn how to kill, and were now making the best of their new task of defending the existence of their people and of civilization.

Next morning, August 4th, we reported to our squadron leader, whose rank in the R.A.F. corresponds to that of major in the Army. What follows will make him blush if he reads it, but I must describe him a little.

He is one of the most impressive personalities I have known. He is slender, with fine wavy hair and mustache, and piercing blue eyes. I seldom remember the color of a person's eyes, but I couldn't forget his. He is very witty in his speech, has a personal magnetism that lends an almost feminine beauty to one's impression of him, and he fairly radiates strength of character and will power. We liked him at once and felt great confidence in him.

He outlined to us the work that his squadron was doing and the tactics they used; and gave us advice from his experiences with the Huns. This was all done in matter-of-fact tones that initiated us to the detached, impersonal, and unemotional attitude that fighter pilots quickly develop toward the taking — and losing — of human life.

He told us apologetically that it appeared to be a quiet time just now. There had been no fighting over the Channel for a week. We knew from the papers that, a week before, his squadron had played the main part in the biggest battle yet fought over the Channel.

"We gave them a good licking that time," he said, "and apparently they've been staying home licking their wounds ever since. We haven't seen a one all week, but perhaps it's the lull before a storm."

He explained that the squadron spent most of its time at this airdrome, its home base, and the pilots all lived here. But part of the time was also spent in shifts with other squadrons at the advance base, an airdrome close to the Channel, from which the enemy planes could be intercepted more quickly when they came across.

He told us the type of German fighting plane encountered most frequently was the single-seat Messerschmitt 109 Fighter, and he gave us some points on fighting them. There was another type fighter, the Heinkel 113, which was supposed to outperform the Messerschmitt, but none had been seen in this area yet.

Then there was the twin-engined Messerschmitt 110 to watch out for. It could be used either as a fighter or as a light bomber, but was considered easy meat by our fighters. The only danger lay in a surprise attack by one of them, because this type carried very heavy armament including two cannons, and if one of them got a good shot at you it would be bad. They weren't to be feared otherwise, though. "You can shoot them down very easily," he said.

There were three types of large bombers used by the Germans: the Dornier, the Heinkel 111 (made by the same company but otherwise unrelated to the little Heinkel 113 Fighter), and the Junkers 88. All these were twin-engined. And of course there was the Junkers 87 dive bomber, more familiarly known as the "Stuka." This was the type which terrorized the armies in France with mass attacks, dropping screaming bombs on them. This type was particularly easy meat for fighters and easiest of all to shoot down. It was an awkward-looking, slow, single-engined machine.

Our squadron leader said that up to this time the only raids had been on ship convoys in the Channel. "But we have every reason to expect," he added, "that they will be sending bigger raids over to bomb our coastal cities and perhaps even London itself, as soon as they get their bases organized in France."

How truly he spoke!

*\*\**

That afternoon we were taken on a short patrol to familiarize us with our new territory, because the next morning the squadron was scheduled to fly to its advance base at about eight o'clock. There we would put in a shift of several hours "at readiness" — staying close to our machines ready to take off at a moment's notice.

I might explain here that most patrolling by fighter squadrons is done under the direction of a controller on the ground who gives the squadron orders by radio. Each plane has a radio receiver and transmitter, and the pilot keeps his receiver turned on all the time. He has headphones in his helmet and a microphone in the oxygen mask that fits over his nose and mouth.

# CHAPTER THREE

# TALLY HO!

OUR LAST instructions by our squadron leader before we left for our advance base next morning were in regard to staying in formation, any time the squadron was looking for the enemy.

"It's essential that the squadron stick together as a compact unit as long as possible, until the enemy is actually being engaged. So whenever we're on patrol, and especially when the scent is good and warm, stay in formation. Fly wide enough apart from your leader so that you won't be in danger of colliding with him, but don't lag behind if you can help it. If you see a Hun don't go after him until I give you the O.K. And if we sight a bunch of them, stay in formation until I call out the 'Tally-Ho!' Then you can break formation and pick your targets. And then," he added, patting us both on the back, "Heaven help your targets!"

We got our airplanes ready and put on our flying equipment. As it was warm, we didn't wear any flying suits over our uniforms, but we put on pneumatic life jackets that were issued to us. These are called "Mae Wests" — quite appropriately, too, as you would agree if you could see what they do to a pilot's contour.

We took off in sections of three and assumed squadron formation over the airdrome. An R.A.F. fighter squadron consists of twelve planes normally, and we flew in sections of three, the leader in front with his section.

It was a tremendous thrill for me to be aloft with a fighter squadron for the first time. We circled the airdrome majestically and then swept out eastward toward our advance base on the seacoast. I was enjoying this, even though it was only supposed to be a little cross-country jaunt.

I heard the whine of a radio transmitter in my headphones, and then our squadron leader's voice.

"Hello, Control! Hello, Control! Tiger Leader calling. Are you receiving me? Are you receiving me? Over." ("Tiger" was the call name of our squadron.)

There was another transmitter whir, more distant, and a cheery voice sang out, "Hallo-o, Tiger Leader, Tiger Leader! Control answering you. Control answering. Receiving you loud and clear, loud and clear. Are you receiving me, please? Are you receiving me? Control over to Tiger Leader."

Another whir and our leader's voice answering again. "Hello, Control. Hello, Control. Tiger Leader answering. Yes, receiving you loud and clear also. Loud and clear. All Tiger aircraft are now air-borne. We are now air-borne. Tiger Leader over to control, listening out."

Control called once more to acknowledge this message, and then there was radio silence as we roared onward. We had to cover about seventy miles, which would take about fifteen minutes. It was a clear morning, and I idly wondered if we should be able to see the French coast that day. If so I should be seeing France for the first time. Also it would be my first view of enemy country, for that was German-occupied France.

Perhaps seven or eight minutes had elapsed when Control called us again. There was the transmitter's whine and a voice calling Tiger Leader and asking if he was receiving him. Then Tiger Leader's answer that he was "receiving you loud and clear."

Then the voice from Control again, this time slower, and with careful enunciation: "All Tiger aircraft, patrol Dover at ten thousand feet; patrol Dover at ten thousand feet."

Our leader immediately opened his throttle and put his plane in a steep climb, at the same time altering his course in the direction of Dover. We of course did likewise to stay in formation with him.

I wondered what it meant. Had something been seen there, or were they expecting an attack? It still didn't seem possible that I actually might see an enemy. Planes with black crosses and swastikas still didn't seem to exist in reality to me, in spite of the one I had seen that spun in at our training base. Somehow that one, a great broken thing lying on the hillside after it crashed, didn't seem real to me in memory. It still didn't seem possible that I should actually see airplanes with black crosses in the air, whose pilots would be trying to kill me, and I them.

In less time than it takes to tell, our altimeters were registering ten thousand feet and we were racing level. The coast was visible now, not far ahead, with the waters of the English Channel beyond. I guessed that we were nearly over Dover.

Another command came through from Control. "Climb to fifteen thousand feet." And then the message that electrified me:

"There are bandits [enemies] approaching from the north!"

My pulses pounded, and my thoughts raced. This was *it*!

In quick response to this information, our leader sang out a command: "All Tiger aircraft, full throttle! Full throttle!"

That meant to use the emergency throttle that gave extra powers to our engines.

I was flying in our leader's section, on his left. As he gave the command, "Full throttle," his plane started to draw ahead, drawing away from me. I pushed in my emergency throttle lever in response to the command, the first time I had ever used it, and my engine fairly screamed with new power. I felt my plane speeding up like a high-spirited horse that has been spurred.

Our leader now led us upward in a steeper climb than I had ever dreamed an airplane could perform. Trembling with excitement, trying to realize that this was actually happening and I wasn't dreaming, I pulled the guard off my firing button. For the first time in my life I was preparing to kill! The button was painted red, and it looked strangely grim now that it was uncovered. I turned its safety ring, which surrounded it, from the position which read "SAFE" to the position which read "FIRE."

Then I switched on the electric gunsight. This projects an orange light in the image of a machine-gun sight upon a glass in the middle of the windshield. It's more accurate than mechanical sights.

We were going forward and upward at terrific speed, and reached fifteen thousand feet shortly. A new command came over our radio receivers: "Steer one-three-zero and climb to twenty thousand feet."

We obeyed, every pilot now watching above and below and on all sides, the sections of the squadron closing in more tightly and the rear-guard pilots wheeling in swift vertical banks one way, then the other, to watch against any surprise.

Our course led us out over the middle of the Channel, and the coast of France was plainly visible — answering one of my hopes. I was getting my first view of France, and enemy France at that.

I was using oxygen now, controlled by a little valve on my instrument panel that released it into a hose connected with the mask that covered my nose and mouth. Oxygen is necessary at high altitude to keep your mind working keenly and to keep you from getting tired and weak. Pilots who don't use it at high altitude tire out quickly, and their minds become sluggish. Also they are apt to faint without warning.

More orders followed. New courses to steer. New altitudes at which to fly.

"Circle your present position."

"Watch to the left."

"Believe the enemy is now heading south and passing behind you."

Such orders as these interspersed the radio silences and kept us busy and on our toes while we hunted about for perhaps half an hour. I was in a sweat trying to look in every direction and still keep my place in formation. Our leader led us about like a group of charging cavalry.

As time went by, my hopes of seeing an enemy flagged.

We were at about twenty thousand feet altitude and a few miles north of Calais on the French coast, and doing a sweeping left turn. Looking in the rear vision mirror above my windshield I saw what looked like a little blazing torch falling in the sky behind me. For the instant I didn't realize that the first shots of battle had been fired, and I had to put my attention again on our leader's plane, to keep my place in formation with him.

I was flying on his left, and that meant I had to look to the right to see him; and out of the corner of my eye I noticed far below and beyond him the distant shape of another airplane heading for France. I hated to call out, in case it didn't mean anything, but it didn't seem reasonable that a British plane would be out here alone, heading in that direction. Also it seemed to be colored blue-gray on top, and I was quite sure no British planes were colored like that. It was too far away for me to make out its markings or even its design. Hesitating to call out, I looked at our squadron leader, to see if he had noticed it.

I saw that he hadn't, for he was looking the other way, to our left, where several distant black dots were visible in the air at about our level. And as I watched him I heard his transmitter whine and his voice sing out the Royal Air Force battle cry:

"Ta-al-ly-ho-o!"

As he sang it he swung his airplane over viciously into a wild vertical turn and laid out for the black dots on the left, which had now grown into airplanes; still little and distant but headed toward us. There weren't very many of them, and the entire squadron was breaking formation and wheeling toward them like a bunch of wild Indians.

I remembered the one I had seen heading the other way and our Squadron Leader's words that we might pick our own targets after the "Tally-ho" is given; and a second later I was peeling away from the squadron and down in pursuit of the lone machine which I had decided should be my target.

I went down in a screaming dive, pushing everything forward — throttle, emergency throttle, propeller control and all. The other had a good start, but I had the advantage of several thousand feet more altitude, and was gaining speed by diving. The wind shrieked against my windshield and the Rolls Royce engine bellowed, while the air-speed indicator needle moved steadily around its dial and on up past the four hundred miles an hour mark.

The Spitfire grew rigid in its course as if it were following a groove. The controls became terribly stiff, and I couldn't move the stick a quarter of an inch in any direction. It was hard to level out from the dive when I got down near the other's altitude. I had to pull out very gently to keep from blacking out too much. The misty curtain kept closing down in front of my eyes as I pulled the nose of my plane up, and I leaned forward and tensed my muscles to resist it. I was still a way behind the other when I got down to his level, but I was gaining on him fast, because of the extra speed I had from my dive.

I was holding my thumb over the firing button now and keeping my eyes glued to the little silhouette ahead, except for an occasional glance at the rear vision mirror to see that I wasn't being chased too. I imagine my heart was doing about fifteen hundred r.p.m., from the pounding I felt.

The other machine grew steadily larger in the circle of my gunsight as I drew closer. I could tell its distance by the amount of space it covered in the sight: six hundred yards, five hundred, four hundred — my speed was dying down a little, and I wasn't gaining quite as fast. He apparently was going wide open too.

Now I was only three hundred yards behind — close enough to open fire, but something made me hesitate. From directly behind, where I was now, it was hard to identify its type. Suppose it was a British machine after all?

To make sure I eased my machine upward just a little so I could look down on the other and see the upper side of it. The old feeling that airplanes with black crosses and swastikas on their wings and sides couldn't exist in reality still had hold of me; but it was banished for ever by what I now saw.

For I could see that the other machine's wings were not curved, with nicely rounded tips, like a Spitfire's; and it was not camouflaged green and tan; and there were no red and blue circles near the tips. Instead, the wings were narrow, stiff-looking, with blunt, square-cut tips. They were pale blue-gray in color, and near each tip, very vivid, was painted a simple black "plus" sign!

I knew from pictures that it must be a Messerschmitt 109, and I dropped back into firing position behind it. My sights centered on it, and I squeezed the firing button with my thumb. *B-r-r-rup-pup-u-pup*! The sound came to me muffled by my heavy helmet; but it was a venomous sound, and I could feel the Spitfire shudder and slow from the recoil as the eight Browning guns snarled and barked their terrific fast staccato. I held the button in for about a full one-second burst — about one hundred and sixty bullets.

Then my plane bounced sideways as it encountered the turbulent slipstream of the other, and I lost sight of him for a second. He must have gone into a diving turn just then, for when I spotted him again a few seconds later he was far below. Mentally cursing my carelessness or dumbness, I rolled over and went down after him again; and while I was overtaking him I reflected that for the first time I had tried to take the life of another man. It didn't bother my conscience.

I caught up with him just over Cape Gris Nez on the French coast, and that was how I entered France for the first time! As I drew close he abandoned flight and turned to face me like a cornered animal; but I was too close behind him now, and I simply followed him in the turn, cutting it shorter than he could and crowding in on him.

I knew I was outmaneuvering him, and felt I had him now. He was almost in the circle of my gunsights. This time I'd keep him there!

*Powp!*

It sounded exactly as if some one had blown up a big paper sack and burst it behind my ears; and it shook the plane and was followed by a noise like hail on a tin roof.

I realized that I had been hit somewhere behind me in my machine by a second Hun, and guessed that it was an exploding cannon shell that made the noise. Most German fighters are equipped with cannon as well as machine guns.

I put all the strength I could muster on my controls to whip my machine into a turn in the opposite direction, then saw that I'd wasted the effort. My new attacker had already flashed by below and ahead, and I now saw him wheeling to come back, his black crosses vivid on top of his wings as he appeared spread-eagled in a vertical turn. The square-cut wingtips of his Messerschmitt looked crude but grim.

He must have dived on me and fired a shot as he went down past. I reflected a little grimly that a new "first" had occurred for me — for the first time another man had tried to take *my* life!

It's hard to recall details of the ensuing combat, but I know it was pretty wild. I made lots of blunders. It was terribly hard for me in my inexperience to try to get an advantage on one of my enemies, so I could open fire, without the other popping up immediately in firing position behind me. The three of us scrambled about in a terrible melee, climbing, diving, rolling, and pirouetting in screaming vertical turns to get at each other. A combat such as this is well called a "dog fight." One moment I would be maneuvering for my life to get away from one who was almost on my tail, and in the next moment I would have one of them in the same kind of spot and would be trying just as desperately to hold him long enough to get a shot.

And sometimes when I got separated from both of them a moment I would see bright flashes and puffs of white or black smoke in the air near me — shells from German antiaircraft guns. The batteries on the coast below had joined the fight and were shooting at me whenever they got a chance to do so without hitting their own machines.

This went on for several minutes, before I finally managed to get one of them all by himself away from the other for a few seconds. I was in a beautiful firing position right on his tail.

Then I got a heart-breaking shock: my gunsight wasn't working! The precious image in orange light wasn't to be seen on the glass in front of me. Feverishly I fumbled and found the switch for it. Yes, it was on. I tried the rheostat which controls the intensity of the light for day or night use. It was on full bright.

It was hard to do this and keep behind the other's tail. He was dodging wildly, expecting my bullets every second, I suppose. I jiggled the rheostat and turned it back and forth, and hit the reflector sight base with my hand and shook it. Still no result. It took precious seconds to do this checking, and the loss of time was very nearly fatal.

A set of four long vibrating snaky white fingers reached across my right wing from behind and stretched far ahead. They were about an inch thick and made of white smoke and pulsated with bright molten-looking objects streaking through them. I knew they were tracers — the trails of smoke left by bullets to mark their course. Chemicals coated on the bullets do it. They show the pilot where his bullets are going. In this case they showed me too, and I knew I was being fired at by the other German pilot from behind. I panicked and rolled into a turn so violent that my machine shuddered terribly and slipped over into a tail-spin — at more than two hundred miles per hour! It must have made me look like an amateur, but it shook off my attacker.

I felt that I was in a pretty bad spot without a gun-sight, but decided to bluff them a little bit rather than to turn tail right away and let them know something was wrong.

The melee continued. I was terribly hot and tired and sweaty, and was conscious of that more than of being scared. I wished I could rest. The bright sun beat down hotly through the transparent hatch over my cockpit. My clothes were heavy and I was hampered by my parachute straps and seat harness straps as I twisted about in the cockpit trying to see above, below, behind, and to the sides to keep track of my playmates.

During those next few minutes I think I must have blacked out at least twenty times in turns. I remember starting to spin at least once from turning too violently. I wanted to flee but couldn't get my directions straight because I was maneuvering so fast. My compass couldn't help me unless I'd give it a chance to settle down. It was spinning like a top.

Finally I noticed across the water, in the distance, a ribbon of white lining the horizon, and I remembered reading years ago in my geography book about the "white cliffs of Dover." Just then that looked like the promised land.

One of my enemies was heading the other way. I made a pass at the second and he headed in the opposite direction from Dover, too, and I turned out across the sea and homeward. It was an ignominious way to end a fight which had begun with such promise, but I thought it was the wisest. My enemies took after me, but when they drew close I turned around as if to go after them and they turned back.

They were apparently willing to call it a draw, and I didn't feel quite so badly after that.

When I went to land at our advance base I found that the trimming controls for my tail were out of order. The wheels actuating them spun loosely, so I knew the cables must be broken.

On landing I taxied to one end of the field, where I saw the rest of my squadron's planes, already down. I was flagged into place, and mechanics and armorers swarmed over my Spitfire. Some jerked off the removable metal covers above and below the machine guns in the wings while others ran up with belts of ammunition and began to refill the guns. A gasoline truck roared up and stopped in front of the plane, and they began refilling the tanks. In a few minutes my machine would be completely checked, refueled, and refilled with ammunition.

My squadron mates crowded around to hear my story. All but one of them were down now, and they had already one another's stories. I told them mine as well as I could remember, and had to admit regretfully that I had come away without bringing down either of my enemies.

We examined my plane, and it was easy to see that it had been struck by an exploding cannon shell, as I had thought. The shell had blown a fairly large hole in one side of the fuselage just behind the cockpit, in the lower part of the red, white, and blue insignia. It would have been a bull's-eye if it had been a foot higher.

The control cables which ran close by where the shell had hit were in bad shape. In addition to the trimming control cables being broken, the main elevator and rudder cables were also nearly severed by the blast. A battery connection was broken by the explosion, and that explained the failure of my electric gunsight. The bottom of the plane was littered with bits of light shrapnel from the shell and there were a myriad small holes in the other side of the fuselage from the shell hole, where pieces of shrapnel had gone out. The shrapnel must have made the noise "like hail on a tin roof" that I had heard after the explosion. My machine truly carried an "after the battle" appearance. It would have to have a new fuselage installed.

I heard the story of the rest of the squadron. They had charged into the formation of Messerschmitts that they were heading for when I left them, and had shot down two for sure. There were also two other "probables" which they had seen going down but which they couldn't claim definitely because they weren't seen to hit the sea. One of the boys had damaged still another — had seen pieces fly off it when he fired.

In addition a Henschel 126 German reconnaissance machine had come steaming along right into the center of the melee, a terrible mistake for its pilot to make, for these machines only have two or three machine guns and can't travel much over two hundred miles an hour, so that they are cold meat for fighters. He must have been going on some business of his own and blundered into the middle of the show somehow, before he realized it. Two of our boys spotted this machine and went to work on it, but they were nearly out of ammunition by that time and they emptied all the bullets they had left into it without bringing it down. It just kept sailing right on, but they thought they killed the rear gunner at least because he quit shooting back at them. It was credited to the squadron as being "damaged."

This is one of three categories into which R.A.F. successes are divided. The other two are "probably destroyed" and "confirmed victories" (definitely destroyed). Only the number of confirmed victories is given out in the report of enemy aircraft destroyed.

The score for the squadron that morning was two confirmed, two probables, and two damaged.

None of our planes that were back was even hit except mine; but one had not returned yet and the outlook grew bad. Two of the boys remembered seeing what looked like a Spitfire going down in flames in the distance behind the squadron at the start of the battle. This boy who was missing was one of the "rear guard" pilots, protecting the rear of the squadron. I also remembered the glimpse I had in my mirror at that time, of something that looked like a torch falling in the distance behind us. When no trace could be found of him and it was learned that no other British planes were missing, we knew he must have been the pilot. There were a lot of Messerschmitts about that morning, and it was pretty evident what had happened.

He must have seen some Messerschmitts coming up to attack the squadron from behind, had turned back and engaged them, and thus, fighting alone to protect his mates he had gone out in a blaze of glory. Our squadron leader paid him a simple but meaningful tribute that we wished he could have heard.

"I noticed," he said, "that we *weren't* attacked from the rear."

I sought out Peter, and we lay on the grass near our machines and basked in the warm sunshine. There were a lot of scratches on my flying boots from shrapnel, and we found a little piece imbedded in one of them.

I felt strangely tired and lazy, not realizing that this was my initiation to a strange feeling of exhaustion with which I was to get better acquainted in the following days. I didn't want to sleep, but I didn't want to move, or talk, or fly, or anything else either, just relax. It's a feeling that's always pervaded me after a fight or a nerve-racking patrol. As nearly as I can describe it, it is a sensation of being drained completely, in every part of your body, though I don't know what of. But you seem to want to just surrender to relaxation, sitting or lying inert and absorbing whatever it is back into your system. I've heard many other pilots say they get the same feeling.

Peter asked, "Will you do me a favor, Chum?"

"Sure. What is it?"

"Let me have your notebook for a minute and I'll tell you."

I gave him the little memorandum book which I always carry, opening it to a blank page. He wrote a girl's name and telephone number in it.

"If anything happens to me," he said, "will you telephone this number and tell her the story? And then —" He paused, and indicated the silver identification wristlet which he wore on his left wrist. It had a little name plate, and also little charms of some sort strung on it. "If it's possible," he finished, "I'd like to have you see that she gets this."

"O.K.," I said lightly, "and let's hope that I never have to do that for you."

Looking at the notebook, I tried to realize that I had bought it only three months before, in a drugstore in Manitowoc, Wisconsin.

I still have that notebook, Peter, and the page you wrote on that day is still in it; though, of course, I don't need it any more because I've telephoned the number and told *her* the story, long since.

# CHAPTER FOUR

# VICTORY — AND ITS PRICE

IT WAS HARD to realize that this had all actually happened and wasn't a dream. This was August 5th, scarcely six weeks from the time I had been at home in Minnesota, cultivating corn! That corn wouldn't be big enough to cut yet!

In England the letters "U-S" have a different meaning than they do in America. Here they mean "unserviceable."

My machine was U-S now, because the fuselage was ruined, so I couldn't fly back to our home airdrome with the rest of the squadron when our shift was over at noon. However, the squadron had a little two-seat training plane for the use of the pilots, and after the boys flew home one of them came back in this machine and picked me up, and I had a nice ride home.

In the afternoon I visited "Number One," our Intelligence Officer, in his office and made out my first combat report. After I finished I spent some time in his office, studying models of various types of German bombers which showed their gun positions and the arcs of fire of the guns.

Next morning when we were collected in our pilots' hut, Number One visited us and passed around some mimeographed papers to us, saying, "Here's the latest intelligence dope for you boys to look over when you have time."

I found that one set of papers was full of information about the enemy's activity during the past two or three days and nights, what units of their air force were operating and where, changes in the status or position of enemy staffels (squadrons) and gruppes (wings), and developments in design and armament of enemy aircraft.

Another set gave summaries of recent activities of the three divisions of the R.A.F.: Bomber Command, Coastal Command, and Fighter Command. A third set proved most interesting to me. This gave accounts of activities of the front-line fighter squadrons during the past two days.

Each squadron that was called up on patrol during this period was listed, and its activities detailed. In the case of engagements the name of each pilot who made contact with the enemy was given, together with a summary from his combat report; and if he was credited with destroying, probably destroying, or damaging any of the enemy this was also given. Our own casualties were listed, with names, and details where known.

These summaries are published every two or three days and given to the pilots of all the squadrons to read, so that each of us is able to know just what our losses and successes are. I have never seen them omit any losses by my squadron or other squadrons whose activities I knew of, nor have they exaggerated our successes; and they never fail to check with the information concerning R.A.F. successes and losses that is given in public communiqués.

You can see that we pilots are in a position to know if the information in R.A.F. communiqués is true, and any fighter pilot will tell you that it is. It was quite interesting and edifying for us to read the papers Tuesday, the day after our combat, containing the German report of our encounter, taken from a German High Command communiqué that was relayed from New York. This stated that we lost eight machines in the fight and all the German planes "returned safely"!

Tuesday and Wednesday were quiet. Apparently the Boche aviators were staying home and "licking their wounds" again.

We had plenty of leisure; and Peter and I visited the "Operations" room from which our orders came by radio while we were on the chase. It was an intriguing and interesting place. In the middle of a large room was a table several feet wide and long, on which was an enormous map of southern England, the English Channel, and northern France. Little wooden blocks were placed on it to represent planes and their positions, as well as ship convoys. As reports came in of new positions for planes or ships, girls standing around the table moved the blocks to the new positions. Enemy planes and ships were "plotted" on this board in the same way as our own.

There was a gallery around the room, in which the control officers sat so that they could see the complete picture of the positions of their own and enemy planes and ships. All the time we were looking for the Nazis that morning our moves and those of the enemy were plotted about on this map. Our controller was able to see our relative positions on it at a glance; and on the basis of what he saw in that room he ordered us about in the air far out over the Channel until we found the enemy!

Daily he played a deadly game of chess on that map, using the pilots as chessmen, with unseen controllers on the other side of the Channel who directed the movements of our enemies.

Wednesday morning some of our squadron cooperated in giving the ground defences at our home airdrome some practice. The station commander had arranged to have a mock attack on the airdrome by combined air and ground forces. We were to furnish six airplanes to play the part of defending fighters, while a Hurricane squadron which was also based here was to furnish six airplanes to play the part of "enemy" bombers. The six Hurricanes were to fly over as if they were bombing the airdrome, and our six Spitfires would attack and pretend to shoot them down.

There was only one flaw in the station commander's plans: he forgot to take into consideration the friendly but intense rivalry between the pilots of Hurricane and Spitfire airplanes. Pilots of these two types of fighters argue by the hour on which is the better, and the pilots of either type never pass up an opportunity to demonstrate the superiority of their type over the other.

Everything went according to plan when the mock attack began. The six Hurricanes which were to take the part of the bombers had left earlier in the morning and gone to another airdrome from which to start on their "raid." Our six

Spitfires went up and began patrolling the airdrome, waiting for the bombers. I wasn't included in the six pilots used, so I watched the show from the ground, standing in front of our pilots' hut. Soon the Hurricanes appeared, flying in good bomber formation, right over the airdrome. The Spitfires went in to "attack" — and that was where the plans went wrong.

Now bombers, when attacked, endeavour to stay close together in formation so that the gunners of all of them can fire on each enemy that gets close, all at the same time. These six Hurricane pilots probably intended to stay in formation originally, until the Spitfires attacked and the full import dawned on them: six Spitfires were going to get on their tails and pretend to shoot them down.

Never!!

As the Spitfires closed in, the formation of Hurricanes literally exploded, in all directions, in the most unorthodox manner for bombers as their pilots broke away to do combat with their rivals, our Spitfire pilots. It was absolutely earnest combat in everything except that they didn't use their guns, and for the next few moments the air above the airdrome was full of milling, wheeling, twisting, diving, zooming, rolling, and gyrating Spitfires and Hurricanes, as the rival pilots strove their mightiest and cleverest to prove the superiority of their respective machines.

It seemed impossible that they could avoid collisions. The din of Rolls Royce engines racing at full throttle nearly made our ears ring. Number One, who was standing beside us watching the show, remarked in his slow, sage manner, "I'm awfully glad that all our boys are crazy. No sane pilot could possibly fly in that melee up there for a minute without colliding with some one!" I agreed with him.

After a few minutes the boys had all had enough, for dog-fighting even in fun is a terrific strain, and the machines of both types came stringing back in, one by one, and landing. Little was proved by it all, because it was such a melee that no one knew whom he was fighting — in fact at times Spitfire pilots had found themselves engaging other Spitfires, and Hurricane pilots other Hurricanes! It merely started another endless chain of arguments in the mess.

It was very illustrative of the high spirit of all the boys. Our squadron leader, remarking about the spirit in his squadron, had said the day before: "It's like holding in a team of wild horses when I keep them in formation when there are Huns near. I'm almost afraid to give the 'Tally-ho' because I know I'll be alone about two seconds later! They just peel off like banana skins when they get the word to go after the Huns!"

\*\*\*

Thursday of that week, August 8th, was the beginning of the German mass air raids on this country — the date commonly referred to as the start of the great Battle over Britain. Of course we didn't know it that morning.

We had to fly to our advance base at dawn, and it was an unforgettably beautiful flight for me. It was just getting light when we took off, and the countryside was dim below us. Wicked blue flames flared back from the exhausts of all the engines as I looked at the planes in formation about me.

We seemed to hover motionless except for the slight upward or downward drift of one machine or another in relation to the rest, which seemed to lend a sort of pulsating life to the whole formation; and the dark carpet of the earth below steadily slid backward beneath us. The sun, just rising and very red and big and beautiful, made weird lights over the tops of our camouflaged wings. We were like a herd of giant beasts in some strange new kind of world. It reminded me of a motion picture named "Dawn Patrol" which I had seen in some other life in another world far away.

We landed at our advance base, and saw our airplanes refueled and ready to take off. It was a chilly morning, and most of us turned in under blankets on cots provided for us and hoped that the Huns slept late and wouldn't bother us until we had completed our night's sleep. We had gotten up at about three A.M.

It seemed like it would be another quiet day. Nothing happened until about eleven A.M. Then the telephone rang, and the call was for our squadron leader. When he finished speaking he turned to us with a little smile and said: "Operations just called to tell us to be on our toes. There's a lot of activity on the other side, and they have a 'fifty plus' raid plotted, coming across farther down the coast. It may turn and head our way though."

A "fifty plus" raid meant a group of fifty or more enemy airplanes!

In a few minutes the telephone rang again. The telephone orderly listened a moment and then turned to us and said, "Squadron into your aircraft, and patrol base at ten thousand feet!"

Instantly we were on our feet and racing pell-mell out to our airplanes. An airman helped me on with my parachute. I climbed into the cockpit of my machine and, trembling with excitement, adjusted my straps and put on my helmet. Down the line of planes starters whined, and first one engine then another coughed to life. I pressed my own starter button and my engine joined the chorus. There was no "warming up," no taxiing across the field to take off into the wind. Upwind, downwind, or crosswind, we took off straight ahead. Better a difficult take-off than to give a deadly enemy a minute's extra advantage!

We roared off like a stampeding herd of buffalo, climbing steeply and wide open. Two thousand feet, four thousand — there were thick fluffy clouds at five thousand, and we flashed up through their misty chasms, caverns, hills and valleys; and then they were dropping away below us and forming a snowy carpet for us to look down on. The sun shone brilliantly above. New orders came over the radio from our controller, much as on the previous chase. Sometimes we were over coastal cities, sometimes over the Channel, circling here, patrolling there, watching for the elusive enemy. I recalled the scene in the operations room and wondered if the girls plotting our positions were any less nonchalant now when there was a real chase on.

Nearly an hour passed without our seeing anything. One flight (six of our twelve planes) was ordered to land, and I guessed that the trail was getting cold. Peter and I were in the flight remaining on patrol.

We were about eight thousand feet up, the six of us patrolling over the Channel, and for a couple of minutes we had received no new orders. The sun was very hot, and I wished I hadn't worn my tunic.

Our only warning was the sudden whine of a transmitter and a voice shouting "BANDITS ASTERN!!"

It was blood-chilling. Our squadron leader was quick on the trigger and led us in a violent turn, just in time. A myriad gray Messerschmitts were swarming down out of the sun, diving from above and behind and shooting as they came.

"Tal-l-ly-ho-o!"

Our leader's voice was steady and strong and reassuring and in that moment filled with all his personal magnetism and strength of character. It was reassuring in its calm call to battle, and caught up shattered nerves and self-control in each of us. He led us together down into the middle of the swarm of Huns, whose speed had carried them far down ahead of us and who were now wheeling back towards us as they came up out of their dives.

There seemed to be about thirty; it was probably a "gruppe" of twenty-seven, and they simply absorbed the six of us. We picked targets and went after them and were soon completely lost from each other. One Messerschmitt was coming up in a climbing turn ahead of me, and allowing for its speed I aimed a burst of fire just ahead of its nose. I had no time to see if I hit it.

My guns gave me a feeling of power. They sounded terribly capable and completed the steadying effect of our leader's voice on my nerves.

Another Messerschmitt coming head-on spat his four white tracers at me but they arched over my head. We seemed to be milling about like a swarm of great gnats in this giant eerie amphitheater above the clouds. Sets of long white tracers crisscrossed the air and hung all about, like Christmas decorations! They stay visible for several seconds after they're fired.

Something about the shape of the Messerschmitts reminded me of rats sailing about on their little narrow, stiff-looking, square-tipped wings. I think it's because of the shape of their noses, and the way their radiators are carried tucked up under their noses like the forefeet of a rat when he's running close to the floor.

One came at me from the side, his guns blazing out their tracers and his cannon firing through a hole in the center of his propeller, puffing blue smoke for all the world like a John Deere tractor! It wasn't a pretty sight. Two of the tracers erupted from guns on either side of its nose, at the top, and two from the wings. It looked like a hideous rat-shaped fountain spurting jets of water from its nostrils and mouth corners!

We meleed about for several minutes, the fight quickly spreading out over wide territory. I got short shots at several of our playmates, just firing whenever I saw something with black crosses in front of me and not having time to see the result.

Then one got on my tail and gave me a burst just as I saw him, and I laid over into a vertical turn; and as he did likewise, following me, I hauled my Spitfire around as tight as I could. We were going fast and I had to lean forward and hold my breath and fight to keep from blacking out, and I turned this way for several seconds. Then I eased my turn so that I could straighten up and look out of my cockpit, and I spotted the other in front of me. I had turned so much shorter than he could that I was almost around and on his tail now. He apparently became aware of it at the same time, for he abandoned his turn and took to flight; but he was a little late now.

He went into a dive, twisting about wildly to upset my aim as I opened fire. I pressed my firing button three or four times for bursts of about a second each, and then he quit twisting. I was able to hold the sight dead on him while I held the firing button in for a good three-second burst, and let it go at that.

I didn't think he needed any more, for I knew of only one reason for him to stop twisting. He disappeared into the clouds below, diving straight down, and although he might have gotten home he certainly wasn't headed right then.

Two more were following me down closely, and in pulling out of my dive I plunged momentarily through the clouds and then up out of them, turning to meet these two. The powder smoke from my guns smelled strong, and I felt good. This was battle royal!

But my newest opponents failed me. As I zoomed up out of the clouds I saw them just disappearing into the clouds and heading homeward. Another diving out of nowhere took a snap shot at me as he went by and down into the clouds, also heading for home.

Recovering from the shock that gave me, I looked around and found no more planes of either nationality in view. I appeared to be in sole possession of this part of the battlefield. This was well out over the Channel and I knew I must be nearly out of ammunition, so I headed for shore and our advance base.

All but one of our planes were already down safely when I taxied into line on the ground. Peter was "still adrift," I learned, and it gave me a little shock. There was still plenty of time for him to show up, though.

We compared notes. Others of the squadron had sent two Messerschmitts down in flames. I couldn't claim mine as a confirmed victory unless some one saw it hit the sea, because it wasn't in flames. We can claim a victory if the enemy is seen in flames or if the pilot jumps out in his parachute; but otherwise it must be seen by some one to hit the sea or ground. Mine went down quite a way out over the Channel (if it went down) and there wasn't much likelihood of its being seen.

We began to worry about Peter when he didn't show up after a reasonable time. One of our boys remembered seeing a parachute floating down during the fight, but didn't know whether or not it was a German. Our squadron leader got on the telephone to try to get news of him. Our shift at the advance base was over now and another squadron had arrived to relieve us. Our squadron leader sent us home and remained himself to try to locate Peter.

We were late for dinner when we got home, and it was warmed over and I suppose that was partly why I couldn't eat. But the main reason was Peter. The chances of good news were growing smaller each minute; but it finally came! Peter had been picked up, wounded but alive, and was already in a hospital. Later we got more details. He had several bullet wounds but none of them was serious in itself, and his only danger was shock and loss of blood. He was "in wonderful spirits, cursing the Huns and spoiling for another go at them!" They thought that if he pulled through the first night he would be out of danger.

The world seemed brighter after that. I thought a lot of this big tough good-natured pal of mine.

It developed that our fight was only one of a series of battles all along the Channel. The mass raids had started, and the aerial "Battle for Britain" was on!

The next day, Friday, we were scheduled to take the readiness shift at our advance base for the afternoon, from one P.M. until dark. In the morning we were just a reserve squadron. There was some activity in the morning but we weren't called out, and it quieted down about noon; looked as if it would be a quiet afternoon for us.

Our squadron leader decided not to go with us and had one of the flight commanders take over the squadron for the afternoon. He couldn't fly with us always, as the commanding officer of a squadron has lots of office work to do, and he wanted to get caught up with his that day. He reassured us though: "I'll keep in close touch with Operations and have a machine ready, and if anything big starts turning up I'll be blazing down there at 'four pounds boost and twenty-six hundred r.p.m.' to join you!"

There was some activity about midafternoon, and we were sent up on two patrols; but our squadron failed to make contact with the enemy. However, toward the end of the second patrol two of our boys were detached and sent to intercept two Messerschmitt 109's that were attacking the balloon barrage at Dover. They found the log's and had a short, sharp dog fight among the balloons and low clouds and bursting anti-aircraft shells over the city. The Messerschmitts ran for it and got away in the clouds, but the boys thought they had damaged both of them.

Mann got a cannon shell in the wing of the Spitfire he was flying and was very worried about it because it was our squadron leader's regular machine. By that time the C.O., as we usually called him, had arrived, carrying out his promise to come down if anything started to happen, and he forgave Mann for it, good-naturedly.

Then while we were getting refueled the main battle of the afternoon was fought near us over the Channel, between other British squadrons and a large mass of Huns. We all stood on top of a bomb shelter trying to watch it. We could hear the roaring of engines and machine guns, but it was too high and far away for us to see anything of it.

By the time we were refueled and ready to go it was over, and there was nothing more for us to do until about eight o'clock in the evening, when we were given permission to take off and return to our home base.

The first thing I did when we got home was to telephone the hospital for news of Peter. It was encouraging. He was still holding his own and doing fine, and they thought he was practically out of danger. I wrote him a letter, cussing him out for lying around in bed when we had lots of work to do. The C.O. told me I could have the following Tuesday off to go and visit him. His hospital was quite a distance away.

We weren't scheduled to do readiness the next day, although we were supposed to be available on the airdrome in case something big came up and the squadrons that were on duty needed help. I got up rather late and learned from the station commander, who had already been in touch with the hospital, that Peter was still holding his own.

Breakfast tasted good. I took stock of the events of the week in relation to myself, and decided it hadn't been bad. I certainly wasn't sorry I had come here. Although I was still pretty scared while on patrol I felt that, given a little more time to get used to it, I'd be all right. I'd been through two good engagements and felt quite sure that I'd already accomplished a little for the flag I was fighting under. Moreover I'd learned a lot and thought I'd be able to accomplish a lot more in time to come.

I was in our squadron office about midmorning when an orderly brought in a telegram for the adjutant. The adjutant looked at it and then handed it to me, and as I read it my mouth went dry and part of my world went crumbling.

It was from the hospital. Peter had had a relapse that morning and passed away.

# CHAPTER FIVE

# DEFEAT

I KEPT TRYING to tell myself, in the dazed moments that followed, that this was good for me, that it would give me the hardening that I needed; and somehow that seemed to help me keep control of my pounding heart and wild emotions. When I was alone I murmured aloud: "I'll make it up for you, Pal. I'll get the ones you won't be getting now. Wait and see if I don't!"

Gradually the waves of feeling grew less intense, and I felt cleaned and chastened, and toughened a little too, perhaps; and by keeping my mind away from the tragedy of it I managed to eat my meals and act normally.

The next day was Sunday, but I didn't get to go to Mass. There were some other blood sacrifices being made, to the ambitions of a hate-crazed, power-maddened little man who wanted to take the place of God.

We had the morning shift at the advance base again, from dawn until one o'clock, and there was quite a lot going on. We did one patrol without managing to intercept the enemy, and on that patrol my oxygen apparatus broke down. It would take a while to repair it, so the C.O. told me I might fly without oxygen if I wished, and if we got ordered above fifteen thousand feet I should break away and come back down.

We had hardly been refueled before we were off again, and as the mechanics hadn't had time to fix my oxygen apparatus yet I went along anyway without oxygen, as the C.O. suggested. We patrolled around awhile at ten thousand feet, then were ordered to fifteen thousand, and after a few minutes twenty thousand. Control said there were a large number of bandits which had gone inland and were coming back out, climbing; and our squadron was to try to intercept them on their way out.

I broke away from the squadron after they got above fifteen thousand feet, but I hated to go back and land with so much going on. I thought that if a fight started it would probably work down lower, and I might get in on the last of it if I stayed around. By listening to the orders the squadron was given over the R/T (radio telephone) I could keep track of where the squadron was and where the enemy must be expected.

I went back down to ten thousand feet, as I didn't feel too comfortable at fifteen thousand without oxygen; and then cruised around listening to the R/T messages and watching for Huns on my own. Suddenly I heard the distant voice of one of the boys in the squadron calling over the R/T, "Many bandits approaching from the starboard!"

There was a moment's radio silence and then another voice: "Look out! There's more of them behind and above!"

Then our leader's voice, "All right! Tally-ho!"

Then there was absolute radio silence and I knew that the battle must be on. I watched all around and above me, but couldn't see any airplanes and couldn't tell where this was occurring, though I knew it must be close by. I wished I could find some enemies at my altitude somewhere.

All at once I saw some puffs from anti-aircraft shells a few miles away and not very high. I reasoned that where there were anti-aircraft shells exploding there must be enemy aircraft, and I headed in that direction, toward Dover. As I got near I saw what it was all about. Enemy airplanes must be attacking the balloon barrage, for one of the balloons was burning beautifully. Great scarlet flames and clouds of pitch-black smoke were rolling upward from it. A furious barrage of anti-aircraft fire was going up on the opposite side of Dover over the harbor, and I headed wide open for it.

The fire ceased just before I got there, and I swung out over the harbor looking in all directions but couldn't see any enemy. Then I saw the smoke puffs of more antiaircraft going up on the other side of town again and I wheeled and made a bee-line toward them. When I got there the shells were bursting all around me and some of them close enough to be uncomfortable, but still I could see no Hun. I got away from there, and the firing ceased.

As I neared the airdrome I saw a Spitfire coming straight down in a vertical dive, from very high. It looked as if it was hit, and my heart sank and I prayed that it wasn't another of our squadron's boys. Then I sighed with relief as it began pulling out of the dive at about five thousand feet and headed for the airdrome.

I was at about seven thousand feet now and losing altitude toward the airdrome and relaxing a little. There were some nice fluffy clouds below me and I would be dropping through them in a minute. A dot on my rear vision mirror attracted my attention, and looking back I saw what appeared to be another Spitfire quite a distance behind and above me but overtaking me rapidly. I guessed that both of these Spitfires were boys of the squadron returning from the fight.

I watched it idly as it got closer behind me. The pilot was doing something which is considered bad taste in following directly behind me. This is bad for a fighter pilot to do because the pilot of the plane being overtaken may not notice him until he is close behind, with the result that he gets an awful scare when he does see him, thinking it's an enemy on his tail. So, normally, fighter pilots never approach a friendly plane from directly behind, but always from well to one side.

This Spitfire pilot kept on overtaking me from directly behind, and it irked me a little, like seeing someone go through a "Stop" sign in front of you. Then when he kept getting closer I began to wonder if perhaps the pilot mistook me for a Messerschmitt or something. Airplanes aren't too easy to recognize in profile, and he was certainly acting like he was going to attack me. He was only five or six hundred yards behind me and gaining fast, so I decided to give him a better chance to see my identity before he got close enough for accurate shooting.

I tipped my plane over in a vertical turn so that he could see the shape of my wings, and the next instant I realized that it wasn't that pilot, but myself, who had made a mistake in identity. He knew I was a Spitfire all right, and that's why he was attacking — his "Spitfire" wasn't a Spitfire at all, but a Messerschmitt 109, and his tracers were reaching out across the space between us! It was too far for accurate shooting though, and I got out of his way and he continued his dive and disappeared into the clouds.

It taught me a lesson, and since then I have never allowed another airplane to get anywhere near behind me until I have scrutinized it and made positive identification.

I didn't think any of his bullets had hit my machine until I went to check my air speed, then I found that my air speed indicator wasn't working. On landing I found that a bullet had gone through my wing, cutting the air speed indicator pressure tube, and causing the instrument to fail.

I had reason to be disappointed because I wasn't able to be with the squadron that time. They had a terrific show, having found far more enemies than they could take care of.

They had first intercepted a bunch of 109's (Messerschmitts) and had got all split up fighting them and chasing them. Our C.O. had shot down one and then chased another most of the way across the Channel, but ran out of ammunition before he got it down. It was losing height when he left it, though, with white clouds of steam and glycol (radiator fluid) streaming behind, and the pilot had jettisoned the hood of his cockpit preparatory to bailing out.

"Orange 55 had got a 109 and then chased a formation of forty no's (the twin-engined type of Messerschmitt fighter and light bomber) most of the way across the Channel. On catching them he "sort of nibbled at one at the rear of the formation," as he termed it, exhausting all the ammunition he had left and getting some small pieces to fly off it; but it stayed in formation and he assumed that it probably got home — "though not in very good condition," he added.

Others had also had good results, and the final outcome, after checking with reports of machines that crashed in the vicinity, was four confirmed for the squadron.

The only casualty was Bud. He was ruefully inspecting his rather battle-scarred Spitfire. A good proportion of one side of his tail was shot away by cannon fire, one wing damaged, and one tire flat! A 109 had surprised him from behind as he was returning from the fight, and had scored a couple of pretty good hits. When Bud heard and felt the explosion of a cannon shell on his machine he had rolled over quickly and dived straight down and got away, not knowing how badly he was crippled.

We had one more patrol, which proved uneventful, and then our shift was over and we returned to our home airdrome. Our C.O. went to visit Peter's parents that afternoon, so before he left I told him the request Peter had made me about his wristlet and he said he would have it taken care of. The funeral was to be Tuesday morning, and I planned to attend.

*** 

Monday, August 12th, was a pretty busy day.

We had one patrol in the latter part of the afternoon without making any interception; and while we were on the ground getting refueled Operations telephoned and said there was a "450 plus" raid forming up over the French coast. I guess we were all feeling a little subdued when we got scrambled again a few minutes later. We knew that if we intercepted it we'd be fortunate if there was more than one other squadron at the most with us in the fight.

However, we were up only a short time when we intercepted a comparatively small formation of enemy fighters, perhaps twenty or thirty. The "Tally-ho" went up and we got all split up. I saw a formation of three that were flying by themselves a short distance away from the rest, and they started going in a circle as I went in to attack, just following each other round and round.

Their wings were different and more graceful-looking than those of Messerschmitts, and I recognized the machines as the new Heinkel 113 Fighters. They were good-looking airplanes, and I remember that they were painted all white. We meleed about a little, and I ended up by getting chased down into the clouds below us, and I lost track of them for the moment.

I was cruising along in a rift between the clouds when I saw above me and to the southeast more airplanes than I had ever seen at one time in my life. It was the "450 plus" raid coming across. It takes those big mass formations a long time to get organized. They have to circle around over one spot for a long time while the various groups of planes get into their places in the formation.

This raid was now organized and was halfway across the Channel.

I wasn't very high, perhaps seven thousand feet, and above me and to the southeast at very high altitude the sky seemed to be filled with fighters. I could see their wings flashing high above, almost everywhere I looked. Farther southeast, not far off the French coast yet, the bombers were coming. I mistook them at first for an enormous black cloud.

I decided I had better get back to the advance base to rejoin the others, who would be collecting there after the fight we'd just had.

I had gone just a little way in the direction of our advance base, cruising along among the clouds, when right across in front of me flashed a Heinkel 113 again, just skimming the tops of the clouds. I opened up throttle and emergency throttle and turned after it. I didn't think the pilot had seen me, because he was higher than I. I guessed that it was one of the three I had just engaged, and looked back carefully but couldn't see the other two. Then I was getting close enough to open fire, and didn't look back for a moment.

*Powp!! Powp!!*

The familiar sound of exploding cannon shells wracked my eardrums and my plane shook. Shrapnel banged and rattled and white tracers streamed by. For all my care, I had been surprised from behind by a second Hun!

I tried desperately to make a quick turn to evade him, but for some reason I didn't seem able to turn, and my plane was just going up in a gentle climb, straight ahead. The firing lasted only a second, but I expected it would start again. I was above the clouds just a little now, and I must get down into them for concealment!

I pushed ahead on the stick — that's how you make an airplane dive — but this time the stick just flopped limply all the way forward to the instrument panel, with no result. Elevator cables gone, I realized. Then I saw why I couldn't turn. My feet were pumping wildly back and forth on the rudder pedals and they were entirely loose too, and produced no response — rudder cables gone too!

This was bad. I could smell powder smoke, hot and strong, but it didn't make me feel tough this time. It was from the cannon shells and incendiary bullets that had hit my machine. Smoke from an incendiary bullet was curling up beside me. It was lodged in the frame of the machine and smoldering there.

My heart pounded and my mouth tasted salty, and I wondered if this was the end of the line. This was very bad.

I could still pull back on the stick and get response, but that didn't help because it made me go up and I wanted to go down, to get back to the safety of the clouds. If I could just get rolled over, I thought, my controls would work opposite and I should then be able to dive. The aileron controls on my wings seemed all right, and perhaps I could get rolled over. My attacker was off to one side of me, out of firing position, but I knew he would be back on my tail again in a moment. He had just overshot me and swung off to the side and would come back as soon as he could get behind me again. There might be a chance to get rolled over first, I thought, then down into the safety of the clouds below, and maybe I could land somehow.

First I jerked open the hatch over my cockpit, so that I could get away in a hurry if things didn't work out.

I had just done that when I was suddenly receiving a salvo from a third plane behind me — no doubt the other Heinkel. The din and confusion were awful inside the cockpit. I remember seeing some of the instrument panel breaking up, and holes dotting the gas tank in front of me.

Smoke trails of tracer bullets appeared right inside the cockpit. Bullets were going by between my legs, and I remember seeing the bright flash of an incendiary bullet going past my leg and into the gas tank.

I remember being surprised that I wasn't scared any more. I suppose I was too dazed. There was a finality about the salvo, and it lasted at least two or three seconds. Then there was a kind of silence.

I wondered if one of them was going to open up on me again.

A light glowed in the bottom of the fuselage, somewhere up in front. Then a little red tongue of flame licked out inquiringly from under the gas tank in front of my feet and curled up the side of it and became a hot little bonfire in one corner of the cockpit. I remembered my parachute, and jerked the locking pin that secured my seat straps, and started to climb out just as the whole cockpit became a furnace.

There was a fraction of a second of searing heat just as I was getting my head and shoulders out, then I was jerked and dragged the rest of the way out with terrible roughness and flung down the side of the fuselage and away all in a fraction of a second by the force of the two-hundred-mile-an-hour wind that caught me. Then I was falling and reaching for my rip-cord and pulling it. A moment of suspense, and then a heavy pull that stopped my fall and there I hung, quite safe if not sound.

I was surprised at how nice and substantial the parachute felt. Everything was calm and quiet, and it was hard to realize that I was only a few seconds out of a battle.

Looking myself over I found that I was even less to look at than usual. I was aching all over, but it appeared to be mostly from bruises that I received from being dragged out of the cockpit so quickly. One of my trouser legs was torn and burned completely off, and my bare leg, which couldn't be called attractive at best, was anything but pretty now. It was bruised and skinned in a dozen places, and there was a sizable burned area around my ankle where the skin hung loosely.

But I could find no bullet wounds. Bruises and burns only — my right hand and the right side of my face were burned too. But it felt so good to be alive after what my prospects were a few moments before that I didn't mind the aches and pains.

I sighed and said aloud, feeling that the occasion demanded some recognition, "Well, Art, this is what you asked for. How do you like it?"

\*\*\*

But I was still in for one of the worst scares of my young life.

It was perhaps a minute or more after I bailed out. I was down under the clouds now. The sound of an airplane gliding came to me and I wondered what its nationality was. I couldn't look up, because of the way my parachute harness held me, and I couldn't see it. I knew that in the Polish campaign some Nazi pilots often machine-gunned Polish pilots who were coming down in parachutes, and I had a little moment of anxiety. Then my anxiety was changed to panic.

A staccato burst of shots sounded, and my parachute canopy quivered with each shot! It lasted for perhaps a second. I could think of nothing but that a Hun was firing at me and hitting my parachute canopy. I knew that if I pulled the shroud lines on one side it would partly collapse the canopy and I would fall faster, so I just went hand over hand up the shroud lines on one side until the canopy was two-thirds collapsed — I wasn't taking any halfway measures!

That changed my position so I was looking up and could see the canopy, and I was surprised that there didn't seem to be any bullet holes in it. Then another volley sounded and the canopy quivered in the same way, and still no bullet holes appeared in it.

Then I looked downward and discovered where the shots came from. Smoke was drifting away from an antiaircraft battery on the ground beneath me! They must have been firing at an airplane somewhere overhead, and the concussions made my canopy quiver. I can laugh at it now, but it was really one of the worst moments of panic I've ever had.

I landed in a little oat field near a group of soldiers, who held their rifles ready as they approached, until I stood up and they could see the remnants of my R.A.F. uniform. They started to escort me to their quarters; when I was halfway there my left knee began to give out, and they carried me the rest of the way. That was the last I walked for three weeks.

They gave me first aid in their quarters, and the boy who worked on me gave me a shock. "You'll get about a six weeks lay-up out of this, sir," he speculated.

"Don't be silly!" I said. "This won't keep me laid up more than two or three days, will it?"

"Well, you've got a couple pretty nasty burns there on your leg and your hand. The one on your face isn't so bad, but the other two ought to take a month to heal. Then you'll get a spot of 'sick leave' of course — yes, I'd make it all of six weeks before you're all fit again."

This was something, I realized. I had expected they'd bandage up my hand and leg and give me forty-eight hours off and tell me to be careful for a day or two — that is, if they were worth bandaging at all!

Several Tommies were in the room watching the proceedings and talking and joking with me. One of them left and came back after a couple minutes with a flask of whisky.

"You want to appreciate this, sir," he counseled. "It isn't every day that a Scotsman will give you good Scotch whisky!"

After a time an ambulance came. I climbed off the cot I was lying on, onto a stretcher that they laid beside it, and they put me aboard. I was taken to a near-by village where they parked me awhile, and then put me into another ambulance that drove for a long time before we got to a little hospital where I was unloaded and put to bed.

The head doctor, an Army captain, looked me over and said that he would have to cut away the skin from the burned areas; and so a cot on wheels was brought in by my bed and I climbed onto it and was taken into the operating room. A nurse pricked a needle into my arm, and then the lights faded. When I awoke I was back in my bed again.

The official British Air Ministry communiqué issued early on the morning of August 13, 1940, stated:

*It is now established that sixty-one enemy aircraft were destroyed in yesterday's air fight over our coasts. Thirteen of our fighters were lost, but the pilot of one of them was saved.*

# CHAPTER SIX

# RECOVERY

I FOUND that all my burned spots were covered with some black dope, and the nurses told me that it was a new type of treatment that didn't leave any permanent scars.

There were three German pilots in another wing of the hospital who had been taken prisoner that evening, who all had burns also. When they found themselves painted with this stuff they raised an awful row, and the nurses and doctor had quite a time reassuring them that it was to heal them, and not to mark them for life! They kept putting more of it on my burns as fast as it would dry, until finally a sort of tough black scab was formed by it over each burn.

My hand and wrist gave me the most trouble, as my forearm, hand, and fingers swelled way up after a day or so and became terribly tender. Even the blood circulation made them throb, and the only way I could keep the pain under control was to have my hand propped way up high and hold it perfectly still. If I allowed my arm to rest down level, the increased blood pressure made it unbearable. The slightest quick movement caused an agony of aching, as did any quickening of the pulse — caused, for instance, by the sight of a good-looking nurse.

There was nothing for me to do but let nature take its course, so I lay as still as I could, counting the hours that went to make up each day. They treated me so well that I actually felt spoiled, though. This was a newly established hospital, readied for the expected invasion of England, and I was the first British casualty they had received. All the previous patients they'd had were captured German airmen.

This hospital was near Canterbury, not far back from the southeast coast, and the big mass air raids which the Nazis were launching usually passed overhead or somewhere near. On the average there were one or two every day that we could hear.

At first the sound would be like a distant storm approaching — just a heavy, distant murmuring and rumbling that gradually grew louder. It still sounded like a great wind approaching until finally as it was getting quite distinct little individual sounds would separate themselves from the rest. The smooth high-pitched moan of a Messerschmitt in a power dive would rise above the rest of the sound momentarily, echoed by the sound of another doing likewise a few seconds later.

About that time we would begin to hear the barking of distant anti-aircraft guns and the sound of their shells exploding. Then as the great storm came closer the guns near by would take up the chorus, barking fast and savagely. Then the raiders would be passing overhead with a tremendous convulsion of sound.

Sometimes they were being intercepted by our fighters already, and then we would hear vicious, cascading staccato roars from the guns of Spitfires and Hurricanes, interspersed with the banging of the cannons on Messerschmitt and Heinkel fighters — terrific outbursts of agonized whining from enemy Daimler-Benz engines in power dives mingled with the throaty *rhoom-rhoom-rhoom* of the Rolls Royces on our own fighters as they milled about; and sometimes the noise of one would rise to an earsplitting pitch as a stricken machine came diving down to destruction.

The nurses would stand by the windows watching and telling what they saw, and whenever they saw a machine come down they would tell me whether it looked like a bomber or a fighter and whether they thought it was "one of ours" or "one of theirs."

For the next half-hour after a raid had passed over going inland there would usually be intermittent activity overhead — individual planes passing over that got separated from their formations, scattered planes from broken formations, damaged Nazis making for home, etc. Sometimes there was a quick burst of machine-gun fire as a fighter surprised an enemy.

More than once I heard a Messerschmitt being surprised overhead. Their Daimler-Benz engines make a low humming sound when they're cruising, but when the pilots open them up quickly or dive them they make an unearthly moaning whine, about the pitch of an angry hornet.

I would be listening to the humming of a Daimler-Benz cruising, and the *rhoom-rhoom* of a Rolls Royce turning pretty fast; and all at once there would be the roar of guns from a Spitfire or Hurricane. That would be answered instantly by the quick crescendo of the Daimler-Benz changing from its normal cruising right up the scale to its most agonized whine, over the space of about a second, as the surprised Nazi pilot "pushed everything forward" and opened up with every ounce of his engine's power to get away. The response was similar to that you get from stepping on the tail of a cat.

Perhaps fifteen minutes or half an hour after passing inland the main body of the raid would come back on its way home. Usually the enemy were pretty badly disorganized by this time, and somewhat reduced in number. Most often there wouldn't be one big formation any more, just lots of scattered smaller ones, the pilots scared and shaken and flying with their engines wide open, and being harried by our fighters all the way.

After things had quieted down the nurses often picked up a few empty cartridge cases on the lawn outside — ejected from the machine guns of fighters overhead.

\*\*\*

Thursday of that week was August 15th, one of the days when the air fighting reached its peak. There was almost constant activity overhead all day. I hadn't slept well the night before and dozed a good share of the afternoon. I wasn't bothered much by pain now. My arm and hand were just as swollen and tender, but I'd learned to keep from moving them and had them propped up high. I was sleeping lightly, and I suppose the constant sound of airplanes passing overhead caused me to dream that I was flying again and on patrol. I seemed to be separated from my formation and cruising along looking for them.

Just then a Messerschmitt opened fire somewhere over the hospital — at a British plane, I suppose — with his cannon and machine guns. In my dream I suddenly saw a Messerschmitt behind me, and the firing was coming from him. Tracers were converging on my cockpit, and cannon shells exploding in my fuselage, and I grabbed wildly for the controls trying to throw my Spitfire into an evasive turn.

The dream came to an abrupt end, and I found myself half out of bed, grabbing at empty air, and conscious of about the most intense agony in my outraged hand and arm and fingers that I have ever experienced! It made me dizzy, and I cried out a little; and the pain continued quite intense even after I got settled back and had my arm where it belonged again, because my heart kept pounding for a while. It was so ridiculous that I had to laugh even while it was still paining; and Nurse Green, who heard me cry out, came in and found me half laughing and half sobbing from pain and weakness — I was very weak from shock at this time. The pain quieted down finally, and I dropped off to sleep again only to have the same thing happen again about half an hour later. After that I was afraid to let myself sleep during an air raid until my hand was better.

After about ten days I was moved to a beautiful mansion near Maidstone that had been turned into a convalescent station for officers. More pilots kept coming in here, one every day or two, so we got fresh news on how the fight actually was going. They all said the same thing: that the pilots were tired and the squadrons at times decimated, but that the morale of the pilots was good and they were shooting down a terrific number of German machines. The Nazi pilots in the mass raids seemed to be very poorly trained for the most part, and scared to death. They all said that they thought the R.A.F. would be able to hold out if the raids didn't get a lot heavier.

My leg finally got well enough for me to walk outside and watch the air fighting from the lawns of the mansion. Most of the actual fighting was too high to see, but we often saw stricken machines coming down.

Sometimes a machine would dive straight all the way in and we could hear it before it was within sight, coming with an unearthly scream just like that of a big shell, caused by the wind from its terrific speed. A fighter will reach nearly seven hundred miles per hour in a vertical dive. It seems that the Messerschmitts, when the pilot is hit, usually roll over and drop off into a vertical dive which they maintain all the way down. I saw at least three or four go in that way while I was at this place.

They came down in other ways, too. Sometimes they would tailspin down, spinning terribly fast, almost like a top. Sometimes they came down in flames, turning and twisting as they dropped, their bodies wrapped in bright flames and black smoke billowing out and leaving a long ominous trail behind. Often, too, they just came in for a forced landing, with wrecked engines or punctured radiators or both, usually leaving a long white trail of steam and glycol behind them.

Although the fighters were usually too high to see when they came over, the bombers often were low enough, and we would cheer or boo the local anti-aircraft guns as they succeeded or failed in getting close to the enemy, as indicated by the puffs of smoke from their exploding shells.

One day some of us rode out to a farm where a Messerschmitt had dived in the day before. It was in a stubble field. There was a hole about six feet across and fifteen feet deep, but the only signs of the airplane were some fragments of the wings on the ground outside the hole. The fuselage, or body, of the machine was farther down the guards told us, and dirt from the sides of the hole had filled in above it. They estimated that the engine was down about thirty feet! The pilot had bailed out of the machine, so they probably wouldn't bother to dig it up.

Looking down into the hole, and speculating on the violence that would cause it to be made in a split second, I thought, "It's a vicious war, all right!"

***

I hadn't heard from my squadron in all this time since I was shot down. I knew that the boys would come to see me if they could, but under the strain of the terrific fighting they wouldn't have time. Our squadron had had little rest even before this blitzkrieg began. They had had hard fighting all summer, having taken part in the Dunkirk battles and in the frequent clashes over ship convoys in the Channel.

I finally received a letter from our C.O. The first lines gratified me, for they related that the squadron had been moved out of the fighting zone for a rest.

He touched just a little on what they had been through after I was out of it. "They came over by the hundred, and we fought them as long as hearts and nerves could stand it!"

I wondered which of the brave lads I knew in the squadron had fought their last battles. He didn't say in the letter; and I felt rotten because I had had to desert them in their toughest trial.

I felt proud, though, because a man who had daily gone up to do deeds more heroic than any ocean flight had remembered to write and wish me well.

I was finally released from the hospital in mid-September and was given two weeks "sick leave" to rest up before rejoining the squadron.

# CHAPTER SEVEN

# BACK TO WORK

THE FIRST THING I did was to visit the airdrome where the squadron was stationed when I was with them before, to get my belongings. I had some misgivings because I knew the place had been bombed; but I found that the officers' mess was only slightly damaged and my belongings were all right. My batman had kept them put away for me.

The station commander and other station personnel greeted me warmly, and it was almost like being home again. I met two pilots whom I had trained with, and who were in another squadron which was now based here. They were having lots of fighting, always against tremendous odds, but were cheerful and happy-go-lucky as ever. (One of them was killed just a few days later.)

There had been a big battle right over this airdrome the day before, and I talked to a Spitfire pilot who had collided with a Hurricane in the melee and had been thrown clear of the wreckage and got down by parachute, unhurt. The wreckage of the two machines collided with a Dornier bomber on the way down and the Dornier had crashed with all its crew, all three machines ending up close together right near the airdrome. He was the only survivor of the three machines, the Hurricane pilot having been killed too.

What a battle *that* must have been!

I wanted to do some shopping and see some sights, so I went to London and took a room in a lodging house, planning to spend most of my leave there. This was a mistake, and I didn't stay long. This was when London was "getting it" at the worst. In the daytime it was all right. Although the mass day raids were being launched frequently, they seldom got over London in any numbers, and when the warning siren blew people just kept watch on the sky, ready to take shelter if enemy planes came overhead — which was very infrequent.

But at night! Well, the first night was far from over before I was convinced that a change in my schedule was in order, as regarded staying in London.

I got along fine for the first few hours of darkness. The sirens sounded shortly after dusk, announcing that the first of the night raiders were approaching; and most of the other lodgers went down cellar to sleep on temporary cots. I displayed my courage (?) by joining the minority who slept in their rooms upstairs, but first I took a walk outside to watch the show. I could hear German planes droning overhead, and there was continuous barking from the anti-aircraft guns scattered about the city, echoed by the distant, eerie *whoompf* of the shells exploding high above. Far up among the stars the exploding shells appeared as little silent red flashes winking about first one point then another in space, where enemy planes were located. No searchlights were on.

No bombs appeared to be dropping anywhere. From the sound there seemed to be at least a dozen Huns over the city, scattered about, but they just seemed to be droning around aimlessly. There were few people on the darkened streets and very few cars about. What people I met were mostly wearing helmets, and I began to feel a little self-conscious without mine. Once in a while I'd hear a little humming noise followed by the noise of something small and metallic dropping near by. These were the little pieces of shrapnel falling, from shells that had exploded overhead. I knew the shrapnel wasn't likely to injure me, as the pieces are small and don't fall very fast; but one of them could give me a good bump if it hit me on the head when I didn't have a helmet, so I soon went back to my room and retired. Few noises bother me, and I got to sleep all right in spite of the gunfire.

About midnight I was suddenly awakened by a distant sound like steam escaping from a radiator. It was a ghostly sort of noise, like something slipping through the air in the distance at great speed, and it was rising in intensity. In perhaps four or five seconds it rose to a noise like that of a locomotive letting off steam close by, and then to a fiendish shriek, ending in a heavy explosion not far away, that shook the building.

I had heard a big bomb falling for my first time! In the last second it had seemed to be coming straight for the house, and after it was over I found my heart pounding and my courage taking flight.

That was the start. It kept up for about an hour, during which I alternately tried burying my head under the covers so that I couldn't hear the bombs so plainly, and then straightening out and calling myself a coward and trying to ignore them, so that I could sleep. Neither method worked.

There was a bomb every two or three minutes on the average. They made various sounds. Sometimes they fell with a long wailing sound, like an American fire siren. Sometimes it was a whistle building to a crescendo; but when they were close it usually sounded like a locomotive passing overhead and letting off steam. Sometimes there would be a "stick" of four or five in a row — the entire load from one machine being dropped at once. None landed really close, but each sounded, before it hit, as if it were aimed for a point midway between the washbowl in one corner of my room and the suitcase under my bed.

Occasionally there was the *ding-dong-ding-dong* of a fire engine as it rushed through the empty streets to some place that had been hit. The anti-aircraft fire was almost continuous, and there were terrific outbursts of barking from the guns near by whenever a Hun got close overhead — which was pretty often. I got to listening to the droning and feeling comforted whenever it got distant; only to be that much more alarmed and tensed when it grew close again.

I tried the old saying on myself that "cowards die a thousand times and brave men die but once"; but it didn't do any good — I was too willing to admit I was a coward! I tried figuring out how tiny was the chance of being hit by a bomb, and that would quiet my fears a little for a minute or two — and then I'd hear another bomb coming down!

I'd have been exhausted if the bombing hadn't ceased after about an hour. Then I went back to sleep only to be awakened again at about four A.M. and kept on nerves' edge for another half-hour or so by some more of the performance.

The "all clear" sounded with the first light of dawn, and it was a heavenly sound. I sank gratefully into a long sound sleep.

I had some shopping and business that I had to take care of, so I stayed one more day. Going downtown I found that several big stores on Oxford Street, the shopping center, had been hit during the night. I think there were some pictures published in America of the bomb damage there. I saw dozens of salesgirls and clerks out on the sidewalks and street, sweeping up broken glass and splinters while firemen were playing streams of water on partially burned buildings that were still smoldering.

That night I didn't get much sleep either; and the next day I bought a railway ticket to Plymouth, on the southwest coast of England. That is a famous resort country, and I had the addresses of some friends there; so I went out to spend a quiet week end and see a little of England. There had been practically no bombing there, and Saturday afternoon when there was an air-raid warning I was astonished to see everyone take to shelters. They weren't used to it like the Londoners — yet. I had an enjoyable week end there and then visited another friend who lived near Southampton; and that way I got to see quite a bit of southern England.

I had left most of my belongings in my rooming house in London, so when I arrived back from my tour early one morning I went directly there. It wasn't far from the railway station, and I walked. About two blocks from the place I found the street roped off, and farther down, across the street from my destination, parts of the buildings were in ruins. Wrecking crews were already at work, and there was the familiar tinkling sound of broken glass being swept up. A "stick" of four bombs had landed in a row on the buildings right across the street from my room, just before daylight that morning! When I went up to my room I found a workman replacing broken windows.

That was enough for me. I decided to spend the rest of my leave with my squadron at their station.

There was a joke going the rounds about that time that applied quite nicely. In England if not in America, would-be slackers in time of war sometimes got a white feather pinned on them as a sign of cowardice. The joke then was about a London boy who left London to join the army, and had a white feather pinned on him. I was in his class; I was returning to my squadron rather than stay in London, which was the real danger zone at that time. I had learned not to mind being shot at, very much, but I couldn't get used to bombing!

Often during my leave I met other R.A.F. officers who turned out to be fighter pilots — riding on the train, walking about London, or in restaurants; and we naturally would fall into a conversation in which each asked the other what squadron he belonged to. When I mentioned the name of my squadron the other would often reply with recognition, "Oh, —— Squadron? Oh, yes! They were down at —— all summer, weren't they? Got knocked about pretty badly too, didn't they?"

And I would reply: "Yes, that's right. Yes, they lost most of their original pilots — about half of them over Dunkirk alone. They're up north resting now, and training in some new pilots."

I found that my squadron had built up a high reputation, though at a heartbreaking price.

\*\*\*

I rejoined my squadron several days before my leave expired, feeling like a prodigal son and wondering if I'd be remembered; and was so warmly received I almost wanted to cry. There were so many new faces, and I found the new boys to be a fine bunch, easy to get along with.

I learned that the heroism of some of the boys hadn't gone unrecognized. Three Distinguished Flying Crosses and one Distinguished Flying Medal had gone to the squadron. Our C.O. had been awarded the Distinguished Flying Cross and there was talk that he might get a bar added to it. He had ten confirmed victories as well as several probables. "Orange," who had six confirmed victories, and Willie, who had four confirmed, also had received the D.F.C. Andy, who had four confirmed, received the Distinguished Flying Medal instead of the Cross, because he was a flight sergeant and not a commissioned officer at the time, and the D.F.C. is awarded only to commissioned officers. He had worked up from the ranks to become an exceptional fighter pilot. He had just been awarded a commission as pilot officer but wasn't living in the officers' mess yet because he hadn't yet purchased his uniform.

The squadron was resting at this airdrome in the east central part of England, too far north for enemy fighters to come. There was very little to do, just an occasional chase after some lone bomber sneaking over in the clouds in bad weather.

There is little danger in attacking German bombers, because they only have two or three machine guns to protect themselves from any one quarter at the most, as compared to our eight. And there is no nerve strain in hunting for them in country where enemy fighters can't operate, because you don't have to be alert against being attacked yourself. The enemy's twin-engined long-range Messerschmitt fighters, the no's, could probably come this far, but we consider them next to harmless as they are very easy to shoot down. The little Messerschmitt 109's, which are Germany's standard fighter, seldom came beyond the center of London, when they came that far.

The boys ate enormous meals, did practice flights occasionally, and rested up for the day when they would be sent back into the blitz which was still raging almost daily over London and southeast England.

I wasn't supposed to fly until the two weeks of my sick leave expired, so I got in a lot of good conscientious loafing. Finally my time was up, and after being checked out and O.K.'d by the squadron's doctor I went out on the field one morning and made my first flight in over six weeks. It was a grand thrill.

That night Andy appeared in the officers' mess for the first time, wearing his new uniform as an officer, with the pretty, striped purple and white silk ribbon of his Distinguished Flying Medal looking very neat under his wings on the left side of his chest. If any one deserved a commission and the right to wear the King's uniform, he did. He had been a mainstay of the squadron all through from the time of Dunkirk, acting as leader of the squadron's rear-guard section most of the time, often with pilots of higher rank following him in his section; and he had certainly "served his King and Country well."

We were all glad afterward that he got to spend that evening in the mess, and I'm glad that I spent a pleasant hour with him in his room before we went to bed, chatting with him about America, in which he was very interested, and lending him some American magazines. We arranged that the next morning Percy, a new pilot, and I would fly with him in a section of three machines to a target range where we would do some aerial target practice.

Next morning Andy had to give a group of new pilots some practice flying before we went to the target range; so as I was badly in need of some practice too I went for a little cross-country jaunt in my machine, familiarizing myself with our present sector of operations.

While I was up I could hear distant voices over the R/T which I knew were those of Andy and the pilots he was flying with. When I heard them plainly I could tell it was usually Andy giving one of the others some order, or coaching them on their flying. I didn't pay much attention to what was being said, but I noticed that when I was returning to the airdrome Control seemed to be calling "Yellow One" and having difficulty in getting a reply. Each section has a color designating it for convenience, and each member of the section has a number, depending on his position in it. "Yellow One" would be the leader of Yellow section; but as there were one or two other sections flying also and I hadn't paid attention to what colors they were calling themselves today, I didn't know who Yellow One was. I assumed that whoever was leading Yellow section was having trouble with his R/T.

The leader of Yellow section was Andy, and he wasn't having trouble with his R/T. Percy ran out to meet me as I taxied in, and with agonized face told me, "Andy and Nels have collided and Andy's 'gone in,' and it looks like there isn't much hope!"

There wasn't. After half an hour's dumb sad waiting around the telephone in our pilots' hut we heard the story. His tail had been sheared off and his machine had gone all the way down, tumbling over and over, and for some reason he hadn't bailed out. Nels had managed to land safely at another airdrome, as his machine wasn't badly damaged.

Just another little sacrifice among the many thousands to curb one man's savage desire for power, of course; but I think for most of us in the squadron the loss of Andy was one of the most painful we'd had to bear.

# CHAPTER EIGHT

# IMPATIENCE

THE DAY we were waiting for, when we could go back to front-line fighting, was a long time coming. Occasionally an order would come through posting one of our new pilots to one of the squadrons that were in the blitz and replacing him with a new pilot for us to train up. Then there would be a lot of good-byes and well-wishes to the boy who was off for the front, including the oft-repeated counsel to "watch your tail and keep your rear vision mirror polished."

But though we grew more and more impatient to get back into the fray no orders came for the squadron to move. I was particularly anxious to get back and even things up for my own defeat. I had no confirmed victories before being shot down myself, and as I told my friends I hated to go about with a score of minus one to my credit.

The great squadron of all Polish pilots and ground personnel joined us, having been sent up here to rest also. They had gotten 126 confirmed victories in less than six weeks, which I believe is a record for any R.A.F. squadron in that length of time. They fought savagely, for their pilots had nothing to lose. Most of them had seen so much of murder and terror and tragedy among their people before they escaped from Poland that they didn't care to live. One night I traded one of my uniform buttons with one of their ace pilots, for one of his, and I still wear it and am very proud of it.

Gilly told me a great deal of how the squadron fared after I was shot down in August, for the rest of the time that they remained in the blitz. The day after I was downed had been pretty bad. He was leading the squadron's rear-guard section on a patrol when they were sent to break up a raid that was forming up over Cape Gris Nez on the French coast. The squadron had sighted sixty Messerschmitts and turned to sail into them, and Gilly's section happened to be on the outside of the turn because of their rear-guard maneuvers, with the result that they got left quite a way behind.

And then the three of them were attacked from behind by nearly fifty Messerschmitts. Gilly alone of the three in his section got back. He shot down one Messerschmitt off Bud's tail, but Bud was already going down in flames, and then his own machine was being riddled from behind, by another Messerschmitt. Steam blinded him so he couldn't see, and he had to open his hatch, unfasten his straps, and stand up to see out; and that way he flew all the way back across the Channel with this Messerschmitt following him and shooting at him, so that he had to keep twisting violently one way then the other, all the time.

Somehow his wrecked engine managed to keep going until just before he reached the coast, when it seized up, out of oil and with radiator dry of course, and he made a forced landing on the belly of his machine with the wheels retracted. The Messerschmitt pilot had exhausted his ammunition by the time Gilly's engine stopped, and he gave up the chase. Gilly's machine was riddled with bullets and completely ruined.

A day or two later Mann got a bullet in his hip and his machine badly damaged, but he managed to fly back to the airdrome. He was still in the hospital and was expected to be laid up for several months. The C.O. had his machine shot down in flames on one of those days, and he bailed out unhurt, although when he landed in his parachute in a small village he had a hard time convincing the residents that he wasn't a German spy who should be shot.

The climax of the week's events was the raid on the squadron's own airdrome. They were on patrol right over the airdrome, trying to intercept a German formation at twenty-five thousand feet, when another big formation of bombers attacked the airdrome from low altitude. The squadron dived straight down at more than six hundred miles per hour and sailed into the bombers. Altogether they shot down ten bombers with no casualties to themselves.

Gilly got one of them, a Heinkel! He got it away from its formation and the pilot must have been pretty good, for when Gilly attacked he did all sorts of acrobatics with the big machine to evade him. Gilly followed, shooting whenever he got a chance, and finally caught him in a stalled turn and gave him a good long burst that finished him, and the Heinkel turned over and dived straight down in from about five thousand feet, bursting into flames when it hit.

Other squadrons that joined the fight shot down eighteen German planes and the ground defenses got two, which with the ten our squadron got made a total of thirty machines and crews that the raid cost the Luftwaffe.

Considering that only a small amount of damage was done by the bombing it was quite a victory for the R.A.F. However, it very nearly finished the frazzled nerves of some of the boys of our squadron, and that night the grateful news came that they were to pack up and move to this place in the north next day.

\*\*\*

Early in October we were ordered to move to a base farther south, which though not yet in the blitz area was nevertheless quite close to it, and there was a lot more activity by hit-and-run bombers. An outside factor unfortunately interfered just then and kept me out of the squadron and in idleness for the first two weeks, but I finally got back with them again and started doing my share of the work. The bombers were coming over individually and trying all sorts of tricks to get us sidetracked long enough to get through and bomb a city or harbor in our area. Often they came over very high, carrying only small bomb loads. The whole squadron was seldom sent up at once, but there were many patrols by sections of three.

\*\*\*

Have you ever made clouds? I have. It was on these patrols that I first made them and became acquainted with the strangest, weirdest, and most beautiful phenomenon that I have encountered in flying. They are generally called "vapor trails" by pilots, and the phenomenon usually occurs only in the thin cold air at high altitudes, although I have seen it as low as eight thousand feet in the winter. I had seen these trails a few times in the summer, when fighters were flying at thirty or thirty-five thousand feet overhead, appearing as thin white lines curving about the sky overhead. Now in the fall the air was cold enough for trails to be made sometimes as low as twenty thousand feet.

I understand that the wings and propeller of a high-speed airplane rushing through the air cause sudden changes in the air pressure in its path, so that moisture in the air condenses into cloud and the condensed droplets then freeze instantly, before they have time to evaporate again.

Whatever be the cause, the effect is the weirdest thing imaginable. As a formation of planes enters the altitude at which vaporization begins to take place, each pilot begins to notice what seem like wisps of white smoke streaming back from the tails of the other machines. When they have climbed a little bit higher these become good-sized clouds billowing back, about the size of the cloud of dust that a car rolls up when moving fast on a dusty road, though of course streaming back several times as fast. Indeed, the pilot's view in the rear vision mirror of his machine while he is "vaporizing" is just like what you get looking in the rear vision mirror of your car when billowing clouds of dust behind you obscure everything else in your mirror.

As a rule these trails stay put for an hour or so, recording in the sky the tracks of the planes that have been there and gone, until they gradually widen out and diffuse themselves in the atmosphere. From the ground the machines, when they are vaporizing, look like invisible paintbrushes drawing silvery white lines across the blue dome of the sky, slowly and majestically; for the planes are too high to be seen themselves usually, and because of the distance the movement seems to be very slow.

To sit on the ground watching the trails made by, say, a section of three planes of your own squadron on patrol, and try to realize that at the head of each silver line curving across the sky five or six miles overhead is a pal who was sitting beside you in the pilots' hut a half-hour before, is in my belief to stretch the imagination beyond its capacity. It's certainly beyond mine! And it's interesting too, to land after having flown high overhead, and to look up and see your own track inscribed up there in the sky.

One bright sunny morning three of us were up on patrol, trying to find a bandit which was reported approaching the coast at a point in our area, and we headed out over the sea. We were at about twenty thousand feet, which is not in the stratosphere, but is so high that the sky is a more intense blue and the sun brighter and everything more frigid and wintry-looking. I had been engrossed for a moment checking my instruments and closing my radiator shutter, because it was very cold up there and my engine was beginning to run too cold. Glancing up, I noticed, emblazoned in the sky far above and ahead of us, something that I could only imagine at first as being a comet. It was a little patch of brilliant silver against the blue, in the exact shape of a comet, awe-inspiring in the weird stratosphere, and it nearly scared me out of my wits.

Then reason came back, and after making a quick estimate of its height and position I called over the R/T to our formation leader, "Bandit ahead and to starboard! He's about thirty thousand feet and making a very short vapor trail!"

We opened throttle and gave chase, but after a minute the trail disappeared, and as we were too far away to see the airplane itself we of course lost it. Its pilot had apparently observed that he was making this trail and had dived to a lower altitude where it quit forming. Apparently the atmospheric conditions at his altitude were such that the cloud formation made by his machine evaporated and became invisible again after a split second, so that his visible trail remained only a few hundred feet long and took on the appearance of a comet. That was the first short vapor trail I had seen, although I've seen many since.

While at this place we got a good demonstration of the intelligence and initiative of Nazi bombing pilots one morning. This was a big airdrome and should have been an ideal bombing target, for there were dozens of big military buildings built close together — enormous hangars, shops, office buildings, big permanent barracks and messes, and dozens of houses for "married quarters." On an airdrome of this kind nearly two thousand men are required. It wasn't much over a hundred miles from the nearest German air base in Holland, yet not a single building had been hit by bombing so far, though I understand that the Nazi news dispatches had had it completely wiped out twice and badly damaged several times in addition.

One morning three of us who were on "dawn readiness" had just finished our early breakfast and were walking out of the officers' mess toward the car we would drive to the dispersal hut when we heard the droning of strange engines near by that resembled the sound of Daimler-Benz engines too much for comfort. It was in the quarter-light before dawn, and the stars were beginning to disappear.

Out of the east and not over two thousand feet up we saw the majestic outlines of a big Heinkel bomber coming directly overhead. If the pilot had released his bombs just then he couldn't have helped scoring hits on our hangars or other buildings, or on us. We waited expectantly, ready to throw ourselves on the ground, but no bombs came, and we gazed almost thunderstruck as the big machine sailed serenely on over. The crew couldn't possibly have helped seeing the buildings of the airdrome as they passed over.

Cosmer, our flight commander, shouted: "Come on! He's going to turn around and make his 'bombing run' coming back! Let's get down to our machines as quick as we can!"

Stan, who was driving, kept one hand on the horn button, and the guards threw aside barbed wire and other barricades in advance of us as we raced through the camp and out across the field. Cosmer was raging and calling the Hun names. The thought of having our airdrome bombed maddened all of us.

"The lousy ——!" he kept repeating. "He's going to bomb us for sure! Oh, why weren't we up five minutes earlier and down by our machines now?" He was on his knees on the back seat of the careening car, looking out the back window.

All at once he shouted: "Look! He's dropping 'em now!" Then, in a puzzled tone, "I wonder where that is?"

Great terrifying yellow splashes of light were flickering against the dim blue sky just above the horizon, seemingly four or five miles west of us, several of them in succession; and after they ceased a lurid yellow glow remained.

"Oh, he's started a fire too!" Cosmer was almost crying with rage. "Come on, let's get in our machines and get off as quick as we can!"

We were at the pilots' hut now, and we dashed in and grabbed our helmets and parachutes. There was no time to bother with flying suits. Mechanics seeing our car racing across the field had already started up three machines for us, and we were air-borne in no time; but we found no trace of the Hun, who had apparently headed out to sea and homeward as soon as he dropped his load. Neither could we find the spot which he had bombed, though after we gave up the chase we circled the area where the flashes had seemed to come from. There wasn't any fire to be seen either. There was a little village, but we could see no signs of damage in it.

An hour later we learned that the bombs had been aimed at the little village, though for what possible reason the pilot preferred a harmless little country village to a big military airdrome I don't know. Fortunately his aim was terrible considering how low he was, and all the bombs landed in an open field near by. The yellow glow we had seen after the bombs had finished exploding, and which we thought was a fire that had been started, was merely from a bunch of incendiary bombs he had dropped along with the big ones. They were burning away harmlessly in the field.

The only explanation that we could imagine for it all was that the pilot didn't notice our airdrome until he was too far over it to drop his bombs, and then he didn't have nerve enough to come back again and take a crack at us. So he just dumped his bombs in the direction of the village and beat it, probably returning home to tell his superiors about "direct hits on hangars, fuel depots, and ammunition dumps." That seems to be a popular rhyme in Nazi war communiqués.

Just after we got back from that chase another section was sent off to hunt for two bandits that were reported over the sea near the coast. One of the pilots of this section had trouble getting his machine started, and didn't take off until the others were out of sight. He was a Free French pilot, whom we called "Chifi."

The other two machines returned after about half an hour, having had no luck; but there was no sign of Chifi. We began to worry. He hadn't joined up with the other two at all, and hadn't been heard from after he took off. Soon, however, we saw another Spitfire coming in and began to relax a little.

It was Chifi's machine all right, and when he landed he seemed to have some trouble taxiing. Then we saw that one of his tires was flat. When he got closer to us we could also see that his guns had been fired, because the fabric covers over the holes in the wings in front of the guns were shot away. He was grinning from ear to ear as he climbed out of his machine, and his halting English told us the story of the squadron's first action in several weeks.

He had gone out to sea in the direction that the other two planes had taken, hoping to find them and join up with them. Instead, after searching around for about twenty minutes he found two twin-engined Heinkel 115 German seaplanes flying low over the water together. He attacked, and in the running fight which followed he shot one of them down and got a few bullets in his own machine, one of them puncturing his tire.

This sort of life was of course occasionally exciting, but it seemed dull to us, with our hearts set on getting back into the front-line fighting. We began to get quite well settled, learned our way to and from all the local pubs in the black-out, got acquainted with the local townspeople, and so on.

One day I received a registered letter in the mail, containing a little jewel case. In it was a little solid gold badge in the shape of a caterpillar about an inch long, with an inscription engraved in very tiny letters on the back — a souvenir of my "party" on August 12. It is the emblem of the Caterpillar Club, to which anyone is eligible who has saved his life by a parachute. The idea is that caterpillars make the silk from which the parachutes are made. It came from the Irving Company, makers of parachutes.

October ended and the great "Battle for Britain" seemed to be abating considerably according to the news, and still we were not moved into the front-line fighting. And then one day early in November it came! Forty-eight hours' notice for the squadron to move to ——, a famous airdrome on the outskirts of London! Jubilantly always, if occasionally a bit grimly, we bade good-bye to our friends and to our comparatively secure life here, and prepared to move back to the battle zone!

# CHAPTER NINE

# BACK TO THE FRONT — TALLY-HO AGAIN

THE TWO DAYS we were given were busy ones. It's always a big event when a squadron moves. While twelve pilots are all that fly in a squadron at one time, it also has its own personnel of mechanics and helpers who move with the squadron; its own office and staff, a hundred per cent reserve of pilots and a fifty per cent reserve of airplanes, as well as all sorts of equipment and spares. The total personnel is well over two hundred.

There was a lot of packing to do and there were lots of arrangements to make, particularly in regard to transportation. The order came on Friday. Saturday night some of us had a little farewell party with some friends in a near-by village, and Percy got tight for the first time in his life and was murmuring all the way home about wanting to get four Huns down before Christmas.

Next day we moved. That was the 10th of November. Three of our reserve airplanes were ready to go (there were six in reserve but the other three were undergoing maintenance) so we flew down as a squadron of fifteen instead of the regular twelve.

The station personnel at our new airdrome greeted us warmly. We were replacing a squadron which had been there through most of the blitz and were being moved up north to rest just as we had been in August.

With wisdom born of previous moves I made a bee-line for the officers' mess as soon as I was free, and "signed in." The best rooms are first come first served, and I got a very nice double room for myself and Jonah, with whom I'd arranged to room. Jonah was going on leave shortly and was to get married, so he'd be living out most of the time; but he would want a place in the mess to keep his flying equipment and some of his clothes, and to sleep nights when he had to be on duty early in the morning.

I was particularly delighted because our room had a fireplace, for fireplaces are the English institution that I love most of all. (This was a very old station that had been established in the First World War, and in the entry to the mess there were on display pieces of Zeppelins that had been shot down by planes operating from here in 1915 and 1916.) There were also a couple of the most beautiful, coloured photos of Spitfires in flight, framed and hanging on the wall.

A second Spitfire squadron was stationed at this airdrome, and I found that their C.O. had been a roommate of mine in the hospital in August. In peacetime he had been a world-famous athlete.

Our first shift at readiness was to be from dawn to one o'clock the next day, which was Armistice Day — of all days to be going back into action!

I went to bed that night with mingled feelings of tenseness and fear, of course, and a kind of a fierce joy. From now on it would be playing for keeps again. Instead of hunting in threes after timid bombers and reconnaissance machines without having to guard against being attacked ourselves, we should now fly nearly always as a full squadron, hunting an enemy far superior in numbers who would also be hunting us and watching for a chance to attack us by surprise under circumstances favourable to hit-and-run tactics.

Because the only type of attack which the Nazi fighter pilots ever carry out against British fighters is by surprise, we had to fly in a type of formation that could guard itself well from surprises and be effective for attacking also. We were shown the newest types of formation used by the front-line squadrons, which while not spectacular was simple and very flexible.

Getting my machine ready next morning, I practically made a ceremony of changing the setting of my gunsight — in my efforts to be nonchalant and unceremonious about it. These sights can be adjusted for the wing span of the type of plane you expect to be shooting at. As you move the adjustment, a gap in a line across the middle of the sight narrows or widens; and the wing span of whatever machine it's set for will just fill the gap when you are at the proper distance behind it to open fire.

Up north, where the enemy's fighters never came, I'd had it set for machines of seventy-foot wing span, for that's about the average span of the Heinkel, Junkers, and Dornier bombers that we hunted. Now I changed it to thirty-two and one-half feet, which is the span of the Messerschmitt 109 fighters.

I also gave my rear vision mirror an extra going over with my handkerchief. The memory of the month I'd spent in hospitals for not watching my mirror was still quite fresh in my mind.

This airdrome was equipped with a loud-speaker system, with speakers on all the buildings; and about nine o'clock a voice boomed over them: "—— Squadron take off. Patrol base at ten thousand feet!"

Three minutes later we were in the air and climbing in squadron formation to the altitude ordered. Further orders followed over the R/T; Control was trying to bring us into contact with some enemy planes that were approaching London. Finally in the distance south of and above us we saw, among some puffs of anti-aircraft smoke, several enemy fighters scurrying about, very tiny in the distance. We climbed after them and they turned back. We weren't able to catch them because they had the advantage in height and we lost speed in climbing; and after following them out to the east coast and part way across the Channel we were ordered back to land. It was a nice little exercise, giving the new members of the squadron a chance to see what the new area of operations looked like and giving the rest of us a chance to refresh our memories of it.

\*\*\*

We had only been on the ground a short time when we were off again under orders to join another squadron and fly with them, the two squadrons together making a wing, with ourselves leading.

It sounded as if something big might be up. We picked up the other squadron at about ten thousand feet over the airdrome, and after they were in line behind us we started climbing. Then our controller's voice sounded in our headphones: "Steer towards Ramsgate and climb to twenty-five thousand feet."

Ramsgate is a town on the southeast coast, a few miles northeast of Dover. We climbed steeply and nearly wide open. It was a dark morning, with the sky covered by a high overcast. We entered the overcast at about eighteen thousand feet, and it proved to be sort of heavy haze, from which we emerged at about twenty-three thousand. About that time Control's voice came again with another order.

"In a couple of minutes I will give you a new course to steer that will lead you toward an objective. There are Junkers 87 and Messerschmitt 109 aircraft approaching this objective."

My heart began to pound as I switched on my gunsight, removed the cover from my firing button, and turned the safety ring on the button to the position which read "FIRE." The news that there were Junkers 87's involved filled me with anticipation. Those are the "Stuka" dive-bombers that were so terrible in their attacks on the armies in France. They hold no terrors for British fighter pilots, for they are the most vulnerable of all the standard German machines. Pilots who have been fortunate enough to engage them usually report that a two-or three-second burst of fire is all that's necessary to bring them down, and they are so slow and big that they are easy to hit. I'd never engaged anything but enemy fighters before, and the prospect of finding something easy was inviting.

Putting two and two together I guessed that our "objective" must be a ship convoy, and the Junkers 87's would be coming to dive-bomb it. The 87's got treated so badly whenever they came over England that the Nazis hardly ever used them now except against shipping. The Messerschmitts would be accompanying the Junkers 87's as an escort to protect them from our fighters.

A moment later we were ordered to steer a course of 45 degrees and lost height quickly to five thousand feet. We headed northeast and began diving at about a thirty-degree angle, back into the haze, and just then someone in the squadron called over the R/T., "Bandits ahead and above us!"

Sure enough, the queer little figures of about twenty Messerschmitt 109's were streaking towards us from in front, passing right over us and so close that we could easily make out details of their markings. It was almost like seeing old friends again. They were painted very dark gray, with their black crosses outlined in white so they could be seen against the gray, and their noses, clear back to their cockpits, were a dull yellow. In the summer they had all been almost white, or light blue-gray.

"Keep formation! Keep formation!" Our C.O.'s voice warned us. "Stay in formation and let them alone!"

I caught on. This was a Hun trick to keep us diverted up here while the raid was going on down below. As these Huns were above us we should be at a disadvantage in attacking them anyway. We kept going downward, and they turned around after they were behind us and followed us down very half-heartedly, not getting close enough to attack.

We broke through the haze and saw we were out over the sea. Far below and ahead were the dim outlines of a long line of ships, and we began to dive very steeply. Our speed was terrific, and my controls were becoming rigid from it. Tiny gnatlike figures were milling about over the sea near the distant convoy, and the air around there was peppered with black puffs of smoke from anti-aircraft guns. A good-sized battle must be in progress.

Our C.O. led us in a gentle diving turn at the last, curving around toward where most of the airplanes seemed to be. It was dull and murky out here, and hard to make out at any distance what kind of machines they were. There were no formations now, just dozens of airplanes scurrying about in ones, twos, and threes.

I strained my eyes to identify the nearest ones, and finally discerned the square-cut wing tips of Messerschmitts. Then we were closing down into a swarm of them and we could see they were all Messerschmitts, and our C.O.'s voice seemed calm and almost nonchalant in all the confusion of speed and noise and emotions as we heard him call out the battle cry once more.

"TAL-L-LY-HO-O!"

We overshot the first enemy machines because we had too much speed left from our dives, and turned back toward them, breaking formation as we did so in order not to hamper one another. Trying to remember to be careful, I kept close watch on my tail as I swung around toward the Huns. In the distance I saw one coming straight toward me, head on. Under such circumstances it's best to keep heading directly at the approaching machine, not giving way until the last instant. If you turn ahead of time while the other is still heading toward you, he gets a good shot at your exposed flank while you cannot shoot at him at all because you've pointed your airplane away from him and your guns point with your airplane.

This Nazi must have panicked when he recognized my machine as an enemy, and that was probably fatal for him. For he started turning away from me when we were still about five hundred yards apart. I could hardly believe my eyes as I saw myself presented with the easiest shot I'd ever had — at his unprotected side. The pilot is protected from the front by his engine and from the rear by his armor; but there is no protection from bullets from the side.

When we were about four hundred yards apart and he had turned about fifteen degrees I opened up on him, allowing for his speed and aiming just ahead of his machine. Once more I was sensing the terrific thrill and sense of power that come from the sound and feel and smell of one's guns in combat.

He kept turning and exposing himself even more to me as we closed together, and at the last I was just firing point-blank at him and had to jerk back on the stick to avoid ramming his machine, and passed over his tail. Just then I saw two other Huns on my right and went on the defensive again, trying to be careful. They turned away from me, and I swung back to see what became of my victim; I couldn't find him and as we were so low over the water I thought I knew where he had gone.

Then I turned back toward the other two, but they were heading homeward and were too far away for me to overtake. I climbed up a little and headed toward the convoy, hoping to find some more trouble. On the way I met three 109's in formation, heading homeward. They ignored me and I let them alone too, remembering that the last time I had attacked three enemy fighters singly I got shot down myself. Besides, I still had Junkers 87's in my head. That's why I was heading toward the convoy, as I thought they would be trying to bomb it.

I had been four or five miles from the convoy when I attacked the Messerschmitt. Going to the convoy and circling it, I investigated and was investigated by various aircraft that I saw; but they always turned out to be Spitfires or Hurricanes when we got close enough for identification. I just couldn't find any more Huns at all.

There's something amusing about the way fighter pilots investigate each other under such circumstances. It reminds me of the way two strange dogs approach each other — very much alert against any hostile moves, circling sideways around each other until they decide whether or not they're going to be friends. Two fighters will approach and start circling each other while they get closer, neither one giving the other any advantage and each ready to change the gentle turn he's making into a vicious pirouette to get on the other's tail if he proves hostile; until finally they are close enough to identify each other's machines. At times of poor visibility like this we are especially careful.

I flew up and down the length of the convoy for several minutes, hoping to find some more enemies, but all I found were other Spitfires and a few Hurricanes, all doing what I was. The enemy had apparently fled completely.

I watched the ships to see if any of them had been damaged in the raid, but could only see one that looked as if it had been hit; and it was sailing right along in its place.

Next day, incidentally, we were all edified to learn from the German High Command communiqué, relayed from New York, that eleven ships were sunk in the raid! I imagine Great Britain would be in a more favorable position in this war if she had ever had as many ships as Herr Goebbels has already sunk.

Finally, satisfied that there weren't any more enemies about, I headed homeward, joining on the way three or four other boys of the squadron who were drifting toward the airdrome too.

Taxiing my Spitfire to its position on the edge of the field I saw mechanics grinning as they observed the tattered bits of yellow cloth fluttering from the leading edges of my wings around the gun holes. This was all that remained of the cover patches over these holes, the rest having been shot away, as occurs each time the guns are fired. The mechanics always watch for this on each machine as it taxis in from a patrol, to see if these covers have been shot away indicating a fight. They are fully as interested as we are in the accomplishments of the squadron, in which they play such a highly important part. Armorers made haste to remove the plates above and below the guns, in my wings, as soon as I stopped taxiing, so that they could check the guns and install fresh ammunition belts. The kid who helped me out of the cockpit asked, "Did you get anything, sir?"

"I think I got a 109, but I doubt if I'll get it confirmed."

Excitement filled the air, as always after a fight. When pilots return from a "show" they are in a hurry to get out of their machines and meet the other pilots and find out what each knows about what happened as a whole, and how each made out.

Each individual pilot usually knows little of the whole of what happened after the leader's cry of "Tally-ho." He careens about, cramped in his little tight cockpit with limited visibility, seeing little of what goes on except in his immediate vicinity, watching his tail against surprises, evading Huns that get behind him and attacking others when he is in a favorable position to do so (and other times too, if he chooses); but like one bee in the middle of a swarm he doesn't get much idea of what has happened as a whole. The fights usually spread out over too big an area. When he can't find any more enemies or runs out of ammunition or low on fuel, or when his machine is damaged, he returns home.

Naturally then he is anxious to find out as much as he, can from the other boys. How many Huns were there? Why were they there, and what were they up to? Was there more than one formation? Could he have found more trouble in a different area or higher up or lower down? What other squadrons took part? How many did we get?

Most important question of all is, "Is everybody all right?" — meaning the other pilots. Often that question can't be answered for a while. It is common after a good scrap for one or two or even more planes of a squadron not to show up at the airdrome; but there can be a numbers of reasons for that. The pilot of one may have had to land at another airdrome, having run short of fuel or lost his bearings in the fight. Maybe he had to make a forced landing somewhere, with his radiator punctured or his engine damaged by bullets or cannon shells. He may have had to "bail out" with his machine on fire or out of control. In any of these cases the news is likely to be slow in coming through. And of course sometimes the heart-breaking word finally comes through that one of the familiar faces in the mess is now but a memory to us and his loved ones; in which case tonight when we have time one or two of us who knew him well can spend an hour or so going through his belongings and personal effects, packing them and sending them home.

That way his room will be empty for some one else to occupy without delay. We try to keep sentiment to a minimum; we're all in the same boat more or less, and he'll find plenty of friends where he's going, who got there ahead of him.

This time there were no casualties of any kind in our squadron, and every one got back to the home airdrome without mishap. Jack and Chaddy had had some shots at a 109, and Jack was very proud of a bullet hole the mechanics found in his rudder. Our C.O. had damaged another 109, and one or two of the other boys had had shots. We hadn't accomplished much, all told, but several new pilots had been brought through their first fight safely, which was important. The whole story of the fight revealed that we were a little late in arriving, which explained why we didn't have more to do.

A large formation of these Junkers 87 "Stukas," escorted by Messerschmitt 109 Fighters, had approached the convoy, and two squadrons of British Hurricanes had intercepted them first before they got to the convoy. The Hurricanes shot down seven of the 87's and most of the rest fled. Only a few got through to drop their bombs. The Messerschmitts then staged a sort of hit-and-run attack on the Hurricanes, and we got there just when they were running.

The Hurricanes shot down three or four of the Messerschmitts too, but they lost two of their own machines and pilots in the last part of the scrap. Jonah saw one of them go down. He first saw it making for shore with steam and glycol streaming back from the radiator, but it appeared to be under control and he thought the pilot was trying to make a forced landing on the beach. Then just as it reached shore and was about a hundred feet up it nosed straight down and dived into the ground and went up in flames.

That was the morning the Italians made their first and last raid on England. It was going on at the same time that our fight occurred but farther south. We had learned some time previously that Italian bomber and fighter squadrons were being based in northern France, but they hadn't made an appearance over the Channel or England.

On this morning, however, a good-sized formation of old Caproni bombers and Fiat biplane fighters were intercepted by a Hurricane squadron. After the Hurricane pilots recovered from the shock of seeing such ancient aircraft in modern war skies they waded in and shot down thirteen of them without getting a single bullet in any of their own machines. The Hurricane pilots who did it said it was like shooting tame ducks.

After that some of the Italian fighters used to fly out over mid-Channel once in a while, stooging around and trying to look fierce apparently, until one day near the end of the month the other squadron that was stationed at our airdrome found them and shot down another eight. That apparently was enough, and a few days later the remaining Italians moved back to Italy. They hadn't shot down a single British airplane in all the time they had been based across the Channel from us, "daily ranging far and wide over England, side by side with the German Air Force, seeking out and destroying the remnants of the Royal Air Force," or something like that, according to the silly Italian dictator.

It was cold-blooded murder to send their pilots up in their little slow, unarmored biplanes with only two or four machine guns against our powerful eight-gun Spitfires and Hurricanes, and they must have been sent for political reasons, like some pilots that were killed in the United States in 1934. I hope the era of dictators is drawing to a close. Lust for power makes even good men turn to doing ruthless deeds.

# CHAPTER TEN

# HUN-CHASING

IN THE AFTERNOON after our combat I saw a mechanic doping new fabric covers over the holes in the wings in front of the guns on my airplane, to replace those that were shot away. "You're wasting your time doing that!" I told him cheerfully.

He replied, "I hope you're right, sir."

I expected to be using my guns often now, but in this I was mistaken. The Luftwaffe was in the process of abandoning the mass day raids, and what raiding they did now was cautious, and on a small scale. The great air offensive which they had boasted would destroy the Royal Air Force and pave the way for the scheduled German invasion of England was entering its final and ignominious stages.

I have often heard doubts expressed that the R.A.F.'s accounts of our own and enemy losses could be correct. The abandoning by the Nazis of these mass raids should be proof that R.A.F. accounts of casualties, which showed that the Nazis lost at least four times as many airplanes as we did, could not have been exaggerations.

At the beginning of their air onslaught the Luftwaffe outnumbered us several times over. England admitted it, and Germany boasted of it. They deliberately announced their intention to wipe us out, as a first step to bombing freely and preparing for and supporting the invasion of England which they promised, and which is necessary for them ever to win this war.

*The Royal Air Force had to maintain an overwhelming ratio of victories to losses in order to continue to exist!* — and in order for England to continue to exist, too, for that matter. If the Huns could have destroyed even half as many British machines as they lost themselves, it would have paid them to continue the mass raids until the R.A.F. was wiped out, for they (the Huns) would still have plenty of airplanes left. The fact that we still existed after the mass raids were abandoned proves that we must have maintained at least a four-to-one ratio of victories to losses; and the fact that the Nazis abandoned the mass raiding was an admission that, in spite of their tremendous numerical superiority, they were losing a bigger percentage of their air force than we were losing of ours. In other words, their big air force was being worn down faster than our little one!

They were starting now a new type of raiding which, while it didn't accomplish much, was far less costly to them. Because their big bombers, slow and unwieldy, were such cold meat for our fighters and were shot down in such a wholesale manner during the day raids, they fixed up some of their little Messerschmitt fighters to carry bombs. They of course couldn't aim the bombs; there was no room for an extra person or a bomb aimer in the machines, and they didn't even have a bomb sight in them.

But that was immaterial in their program of terrorizing the civilians of London, for London is so big and thickly populated that they didn't have to aim the bombs — if they just flew anywhere over the city and dropped them, there was a good chance of killing some people. Each plane so equipped usually carried a 550-pound bomb under its belly. The weight and wind resistance of the bomb of course impaired the performance of the Messerschmitts, but they were still much faster than any regular bombers, and being small they weren't as easy for us to spot when we were hunting for them. Also, once they had released their bombs, they had all their original performance back again and had just as much chance to race or fight their way home as any other fighter. They carried their regular machine guns and cannon just the same when they were carrying bombs as otherwise. In case they were intercepted before they reached their objective they jettisoned their bombs wherever they were, so that they'd have a better chance to get away without fighting, or could fight better if they had to fight.

So now we were often sent up to chase "Messerschmitt 109 bombers." Chasing them was easier than catching them, for they were very careful about it, coming over only when conditions were favorable for them to get through to London without having to fight. They flew at twenty-two or twenty-three thousand feet, usually, which seemed to be as high as they could get when carrying bombs; and they were often escorted by others without bombs, flying above them at any altitude up to thirty-five thousand feet.

Both the British and the Germans have listening devices on their respective sides of the Channel, by which each side can tell when an enemy formation is flying on the opposite side, if it's anywhere near the coast; and they can keep track of its position and height. As soon as a formation of Messerschmitts would take off on the other side (all the fighter airdromes are near the coast) one or more of our squadrons would be sent up on patrol to be ready to intercept them if they came across. The Nazis of course kept track of the positions of our squadrons; and if our machines seemed to be in a good position to intercept their planes the Nazi controllers would order their pilots (by radio) not to start across.

Then they'd just fly up and down the French coast, and we'd fly up and down the English coast, "figuratively glaring at each other across the Channel," as I said in one of my letters home at about that time. They'd be hoping that we'd get sidetracked long enough for them to make a dash across and get by us; and we would sit up there hoping they'd try it. They got to using all sorts of tricks, sending over several small formations at a time at different points to draw us off guard, playing hide and seek in the clouds, and leading us all sorts of merry chases.

For example, one afternoon we were scrambled and ordered to patrol over Canterbury at fifteen thousand feet. Canterbury is a fairly large place a few miles from the coast, and is a handy point to stay around because it is easy to see and keep track of when pilots are busier watching the sky above than the ground below. After we'd hung around over there a few minutes Control called and said, "Steer a course of 150 degrees and climb to twenty-three thousand feet. There are several bandits approaching Dungeness from Boulogne at about that altitude."

Our leader acknowledged the message and we went roaring out toward Dungeness, our gunsights switched on, firing buttons off safety, and blood in our eyes, I suppose.

We steamed out over Dungeness, our C.O. anxiously calling Control. "Can you tell me where the bandits are now? We are circling Dungeness but can't see anything."

Control's voice answered: "Sorry, they must have smelled you. They've turned back again. Steer three six zero. There is another formation of about fifteen bandits now approaching Manston from Cape Gris Nez at about your altitude."

We turned northward as ordered, and as we approached Manston Control called out: "Be careful. Keep a sharp lookout above! There may be more bandits very high above them!"

This was the warning for all of us to watch the sky above for vapor trails. We weren't "vaporizing" at our present altitude, but airplanes very much above us probably would be.

A moment later one of our boys called out, "Vapor trails above and starboard!"

I looked carefully, and then I saw them, about twenty eerie little silver lines crawling across the sky above from the southeast, close together. They were undoubtedly the trails of Messerschmitts without bombs, flying at thirty or thirty-five thousand feet in the stratosphere, supposedly to protect those lower down which we were searching for and which would be carrying bombs.

We couldn't bother about those high ones now. If they wanted to come down to our level and fight, O.K., but we weren't going to climb up after them when there were others at our own altitude. Our rear guard would keep close watch on them so they couldn't pull a surprise attack from above. We kept going straight and level towards Manston, and when we got there Control called and said: "Sorry again! They are getting very careful. The bandits which were at your altitude have turned back. You may use your discretion about the ones above you." The vapor trails were almost directly over us now.

Our C.O. answered Control: "Thank you. I think we'll climb up and try to have a go at them."

And heading southwest to get us out from under them he led us upward in a steep climb to try to reach their altitude. Soon it grew very cold in our cockpits, as our altimeter needles approached the thirty-thousand-foot mark on their dials. I could see the fluffy cloud trails streaming back from each of the other planes in the formation, for of course we were making vapor trails ourselves now. The Huns above, after making a big circle, had turned north now, and we did likewise, following them and climbing. They were still some distance above us. As we got farther up in the stratosphere the sky grew a more intense blue, and the sun was weirdly bright and wintry. We climbed on above thirty thousand.

The air at that altitude is so thin that even these high-powered machines lose most of their beautiful flying qualities. Controls work very easily and the airplane responds to them only sluggishly, as a car responds to the steering wheel on ice, instead of with the rigid alertness one gets accustomed to in these machines at normal altitudes. The powerful engine becomes lazy too. Somehow the air one is riding on feels terribly unsubstantial, and until one gets used to it he gets a feeling of insecurity, a feeling that he and his machine are on the verge of losing what little support the air gives up there, and just falling off into the eerie, seemingly limitless space below. The ground seems as far away as a distant continent, and he wonders if he will ever find his way back.

Visibility is unbelievable in the thin air up there. If there are no clouds below it isn't uncommon to see the whole of southeast England, northeast France, and Belgium, as well as the sea in between, just like looking at a map.

We could watch our enemies by their vapor trails, and they likewise could watch us; and as we drew near their altitude they turned southeast and headed homeward. We tried to head them off, but they had too much of a start. It is very hard to fight with an unwilling enemy.

These German attacks by bomb-carrying fighters began about mid-October, I believe, and were more or less abandoned by the first of December. They had become less and less successful and more and more expensive to themselves as our controllers and squadron leaders became experienced in combating them. Our squadron intercepted one of the last ones they attempted.

We were on patrol one morning at about twenty-two or twenty-three thousand feet, having chased around quite a bit after raids that started across the Channel and then turned back. We were right over Dungeness, heading about straight east, our only recent information being that "there are several bandits somewhere in your vicinity."

Suddenly one of our new pilots who hadn't had a fight yet called out on the R/T, in a very subdued voice that we all laughed about afterwards, "Bandits coming up on the starboard!"

And there they were, little ratlike log's streaking across so that they passed just under us, going at right angles to our course. If they had been two hundred feet higher we'd have collided with them! They had simply blundered into us, and we into them.

Our C.O. shouted a quick "Tally-ho!" and the squadron exploded in all directions. So did the Hun formation. I didn't get to see it, but the boys who were closest to the 109's saw them let their bombs go — a dozen or so big bombs jettisoned to fall harmlessly on the beaches of Dungeness.

The Messerschmitts were scattering and diving, and it was more or less of a hide-and-seek proposition to find them. I didn't get a single shot. After hunting around for two or three minutes I gave up trying to find any of them as they had quite obviously taken the shortest route home.

However, I could see three or four pairs of vapor trails scattered about the sky higher up, all coming inland, and I decided to try to stalk one pair of them, climbing to a higher level and getting "up sun" of them. I was getting along pretty well, when looking above me in the other direction I saw the vapor trails of two others that were stalking me, and were just getting to a good position to attack. I panicked a little then and dived away from them, making the excuse to myself that

I couldn't do anything but get hurt if I stayed up there with these two getting ready to take a crack at me.

Returning to our base, I found that once again the squadron had had no casualties and a little had been accomplished. Our C.O. had shot one Messerschmitt down into the sea for his eleventh confirmed victory, and one other pilot had damaged another 109. Our C.O. had also gone back up, the same as I did, to stalk one of the pairs that came over higher, and he got "jumped" by two Heinkel 113 fighters and had the sliding hatch over his cockpit shot away!

***

I took forty-eight hours' leave shortly after that, and spent it shopping in London. There was little bombing in London now, and the city had recovered quite well from the bombings it had undergone in the fall. I had a very pleasant and interesting time walking about and shopping and seeing the thousands of historical sights. I got some genuine English plum puddings, or Christmas puddings, and sent them to my folks for Christmas presents.

When I got back to the squadron I found that I had missed a spot of action with them, in which they hadn't fared so well. They had chased after some Messerschmitts among cloud and fog over the Channel and some of them got separated from the squadron. Chaddy found a 109 and damaged it and got shot up by another and had to make a forced landing with his engine wrecked by cannon shells.

"Hop" didn't come back. The last they saw of him he was diving in among some scattered clouds after some 109's that he had spotted, shouting "Tally-ho" over his R/T. No one ever found out what became of him; but we felt pretty sure that, however they got him, they knew they had a job on their hands before he went down.

With the end of November I had had three more weeks of "front-line" service since we moved to this airdrome, and as yet I had only used my guns the one time. I wasn't very proud of that record, but it was as much as most of the rest had done. Of course the weather interfered a lot, keeping both sides on the ground a good share of the time. But the Huns just weren't fighting anyway. They liked to come over our territory whenever they got a chance, but they avoided combat when they did so.

We had had only two fights so far, and for the amount of patrolling we did we could have had a dozen if the Nazis had shown the slightest desire to really tangle with us. We were still on the defensive, to be true. We never went over France, just waited for the Huns to come over our side, because we weren't big enough for offensive fighting yet. The patrolling we did, hunting for them, was often enjoyable though, because of the magnificent scenery where we flew, high among the beautiful and ever different cloud formations. Then there were the striking and unforgettable views we often got of British or German formations making their beautiful vapor trails in the cold blue stratosphere.

Because their bomb-carrying fighters were having so little success the Huns practically abandoned their use about the first of December, and after that they just sent over formations of ordinary fighters on what we term "offensive patrols."

Most of the time they kept one or more formations on patrol high up over their own side. It didn't pay us to keep a patrol in the air to guard against them all the time, so sometimes when none of our squadrons were aloft one of these high-flying patrols would come over our side, usually at from thirty to thirty-five thousand feet, making what's called an "offensive sweep." One or more of our squadrons would then be sent aloft in an effort to intercept them, or to at least drive them home.

The German strategy was to try to get around above us while we were climbing up to intercept them, and then to dive on the rear of our formation. Because we were climbing we wouldn't be going ahead very fast, while the Huns, by diving, could gain terrific speed by the time they reached us, take a shot as they went past, and scuttle for home without our being able to stop them. It was a tip-and-run method that involved little danger for them, although it couldn't accomplish much either. It didn't work very often, just once in a while at first, until the squadrons learned how to guard against it. Our squadron was never jumped that way, although we came close to it on two or three occasions.

Guarding against this tactic was mainly up to the top "weaver" of each of our formations. He had to be alert and watching the sky above and behind all the time. As a rule the job of rear guard was rotated among us, a different pair of pilots doing the job each day. I liked it myself, and I always got a thrill, knowing that they were depending on me to warn them against danger from above and behind. Only once did I come close to getting into trouble at it.

We were up quite high that morning, and my own altimeter was showing thirty-four thousand feet where I was, about a thousand feet above the rest of the squadron. We were hunting for some Huns that were reported to be at about thirty thousand feet, but we were flying a little higher than that so as to have the jump on them if we found them. The squadron was heading north, about over the Thames Estuary, and all the boys were of course making beautiful vapor trails below me.

It was strange trying to realize that each of those weird moth-shaped, beautifully camouflaged creatures plummeting along and spurning back its vapor trail below me in this eerie frigid stratosphere was piloted by a pal of mine. Up in front was our C.O., who had visited the Air Ministry a day or so previously and afterwards told me that he thought he could arrange for me to get back to America on leave soon. Just behind him and to the side was Percy, who would be practising with me on our accordions in my room in the mess in the afternoon.

Jonah, who kept some of his things in my room and often slept there, was number three in the formation below. Ewan, who had had me home with him at his parents' magnificent old place in Buckinghamshire a few days before, was number eight. I could think of something intimate about each of the boys, yet now they looked like characters from some book about the distant future when I swooped low enough over their machines to make out their weirdly helmeted and goggled and masked heads beneath the transparent hoods over their cockpits; and I suppose

I looked just as weird and distant to them, back over them and leaving my own vapor trail.

I was disturbed from these reflections by the sight of four vapor trails coming from the west and about a thousand feet above me. I called a warning to the squadron and then continued keeping the vapor trails under careful watch as they came closer. I had been on the right-hand leg of my course across the squadron and was just swinging toward the vapor trails when they got right overhead; and rather than lose sight of them by turning back I just continued my left turn until I had circled clear around and was headed south, in the opposite direction from the squadron. I could see the planes making the trails above, plainly, and recognized them as Messerschmitt 109's; and I was pretty scared for a minute because I was getting far away behind the squadron and giving these Huns just what they were looking for — a chance to drop on a straggler, the straggler being me.

Accordingly I kept turning directly toward them as they passed over, so that when they came down at me they would have to meet me head on, which would give them the poorest possible shot and would give me a chance to shoot back at them. To my surprise they didn't come down at me, and I never did know why. Probably they felt that as long as I obviously saw them and was facing them they wouldn't have a very good chance of getting me. They kept going straight on, and for a few seconds I was afraid to turn back toward the squadron, thinking this was a trick and they would come after me as soon as I turned tail.

When I did turn I tried to rush it too quickly and threw my plane into a tailspin, losing a thousand feet or so and looking like a complete amateur. The squadron was out of sight by this time, but I was able to track it down by the vapor trails and rejoined the rest after two or three minutes!

\*\*\*

One morning about the 10th of December a beautiful piece of combined controlling and squadron leading enabled the other Spitfire squadron which was stationed at our airdrome (the same squadron which shot down the eight Italians) to carry out a perfect interception on a formation of these high-flying Messerschmitts. They got above and up sun of them, dropped on them, and shot down eight without a single casualty among themselves.

A few days later one of their pilots received a present of an Iron Cross, forwarded to him from a German prisoner. It developed that this German was one of the eight who had been shot down that morning, and had force-landed his machine in Kent. When police came to take him prisoner they found him grinding something into the ground with his heel. It was his Iron Cross. He explained to interrogators that he thought the British would shoot any German they captured who had such a decoration. When he was told that he was mistaken, that the British respect bravery among their foes as well as their own men, he was so relieved and impressed that he asked that they give his Iron Cross to the pilot who had shot him down — as a token of respect. They checked up, determined which pilot had shot the boy down, and sent it to him.

That is only one of many examples of the illusions which especially the younger Nazi pilots have. Frequently these boys, on being captured in England, insisted on being taken to the nearest German Army headquarters — it was useless for their captors to lie to them, they knew that all of England except London and a few other isolated areas was in German hands!

Our squadron had a good chase one day when I was off duty about this time. They were up hunting for some Messerschmitt log's, and one of the boys sighted one of the twin-engined long-range no's flying high above them. It was apparently over on reconnaissance work, the crew hoping to get through to take some pictures and get back safely by flying as high as possible. The squadron was at about thirty thousand feet and this machine was about thirty-five thousand. It turned and started to flee homeward at sight of our squadron.

Our C.O., sizing up the situation, called over the R/T: "All right, boys! It's a free-for-all. Break formation and go get him!"

The result, according to the boys, was a perfect aerial fox-hunt. It developed that Trevor had the most powerful machine and was soon leading the pack. He gained on the Hun fast, and when they were out to sea a ways he finally got within shooting range. The rest of the squadron machines were keeping up as far as distance was concerned, but they weren't high enough yet. They were mostly right below Trevor.

Trevor opened up with a good burst from his guns, and the 110 immediately went into an evasive dive. That was fatal, for then the rest of the boys were able to pounce on him. Nearly everyone had a shot as the Hun was going down, and they practically shot him to pieces by the time he hit the sea. The victory was finally divided among the three pilots who had shot the most ammunition, each being credited with one-third of a victory!

\*\*\*

The high-flying "offensive patrols" by the enemy also petered out about mid-December, and for the next three weeks there was almost nothing for us to do, the only daylight enemy activity being lone "snooping" bombers which came over occasionally in clouds or fog. Usually two or three planes took off when one of them came over; but as the work was divided among the nearly two dozen front-line squadrons the average of us weren't up more than once or twice a week. All through from mid-November on, in fact, the weather was so often bad that we had lots of time off.

As a rule we were scheduled to be "at readiness" about half the time — either from dawn until lunch or from lunch until dark, each day. But when the weather was bad our readiness state would be changed so that we could stay in the mess, provided we were dressed and ready to go quickly and had a car waiting for us outside; or at times we would be "available at call," in which case we could be anywhere on the camp, or could stay in bed if we liked.

Toward the end of December things were so quiet that we were often released for the day. Then if it was early enough to make it worth while I usually walked over to the railway station and went downtown. The electric line was just a few minutes' walk from the mess, and the trains ran every twenty minutes.

I never got tired of walking about London and exploring. After dark I usually took in a movie before going home. It was often strange to be all engrossed in an American movie and completely lost in the American atmosphere, and then be reminded of where I was by the muffled booming of anti-aircraft guns opening up at the first night raider of the evening; and I'd wonder absently if it was going to be "blitzy going home" tonight.

This was altogether one of the easiest periods of my life. There was practically no work, and the flying we did was just enough to put a tang into the existence, like hunting on Sunday afternoon.

There was seldom any bombing in the vicinity of our airdrome, although the Huns passed over at night frequently; and some evenings there was a pretty continuous racket from the anti-aircraft guns around. There was one battery of three very heavy guns only a short distance from the mess, which we referred to as "Alfy." As a rule Alfy didn't waste shots, his shots being expensive, and he only fired at high-flying aircraft and then not very often at night. We were glad of that. We didn't mind the other guns around, which weren't as big and were farther away so that their noise didn't bother us. But when Alfy spoke everyone in the mess jumped. It was a terrific *blam!!* repeated three times in quick succession, and the windows and doors would rattle and slam shut, and after our ears stopped ringing we'd hear a sighing sound as the three shells rocketed skyward. Then, seemingly a long time afterward, would come the distant, heavy *whoompf! ... whoompf-whoompf!* of the shells exploding far above.

I have seen Alfy, in daylight, put a shell up right beside a German reconnaissance machine that was over thirty thousand feet high. I know it was that high; I was up there chasing it.

# CHAPTER ELEVEN

# A DAY AT WAR

I'LL TRY to take you through just an average sort of day such as I passed during this quiet period of the war, to give you a little more insight into the kind of life we lead over here.

The day begins with my elderly batman waking me up by coming into my room at about six-thirty to get my uniform, shoes, and flying boots. I hear him moving about, and when he sees that I'm awake he asks, "What time do ye want calling, sir? 55

The squadron is scheduled for morning readiness today, but if the weather is bad we shall probably get changed to available at call, so I ask in return, "What's the weather like?"

"Well, I cahn't tell very good, sir; 't's pretty dark yet, I wouldn't think it's so bad though.'Tain't mistin' or anything."

"O.K.," I say. "Make it about seven-thirty, will you?" And I drowse off, scarcely hearing his "Very good, sir."

I rouse slightly when he brings my uniform, shoes, and boots back in after polishing the buttons on the former and shining the latter; then I sink back to sleep again, to be wakened by his voice saying: "It's seven-thirty now, sir. Weather seems to be all right outside."

I rouse, wash, shave, and dress.

During the day pilots are allowed to depart a little from specified dress. We don't wear collars or ties ordinarily, because they hamper us in looking around in the air; and we usually wear roll-neck sweaters except in warm weather. We wear our heavy fur-lined flying boots instead of shoes, with the bottoms of our trousers tucked into them and perhaps a map or two stuck in there also. That's the handiest place to carry our maps.

Dressed, I walk down the hallway to the large dining hall, where other pilots of the squadron are drifting in, clomping with their big boots and rubbing their eyes sleepily. To make sure of the weather a few of us take a look outside. It's still dark, for England is much farther north than the United States and the nights are very long in winter. We see some stars shining, so we know the weather is probably going to be all right and we shan't get out of doing our readiness.

Copies of all the morning London papers are laid out on a table in one corner of the dining hall, and as we come into the hall some of us pick up copies to read while we're eating breakfast. We bid one another sleepy good mornings, and read, chat, and trade papers while we're eating. Breakfast consists as usual of cereal, bacon and eggs, toast, marmalade, and tea.

Just we pilots and the cooks and waiters are up. The ground personnel don't get up this early ordinarily, and the pilots of the other squadron, who don't go on readiness until this afternoon, will sleep later yet.

Breakfast over, it is time to get going, and we get our jackets and caps from the hallway and troop outside to the big old lorry waiting for us. Among the assortment of flying suits issued to each of us is a very heavy two-piece fur-lined leather affair, consisting of jacket and trousers, called an "Irving suit." While few of us ever use the trousers, most boys like to wear the jackets about the camp on cold days as well as in the air sometimes; so most of us are wearing these heavy brown Irving jackets.

We pile into the waiting lorry, laughing and joking and helping each other up; and after we're all in Pip remembers that he left his goggles in his room where he was repairing the strap on them last night, and has to go back after them.

Finally we get going and drive through between the darkened buildings on the airdrome, across the parade ground, and to the sergeants' mess. After a wait of a minute or so half a dozen sergeant pilots come trooping out, munching pieces of toast and pulling on their Irving jackets as they come. About a third of the pilots in the R.A.F. are sergeants.

The gray of approaching dawn is showing in the east as we drive past the great looming dark hangars and skirt the edge of the field going around to our flight headquarters. A squadron is divided into two flights, A Flight and B Flight, and while in some places both flights share the same headquarters we had separate headquarters here, located at some distance from each other along the edge of the field.

We can hear the bellowing of a Spitfire's Rolls Royce engine at full throttle, getting its morning "run-up" as we near B Flight's headquarters. We pass in front of the airplane, a big ghostly shape dimly visible in its parking space, its propeller forming a filmy gray disk and bright blue and yellow flames ripping back from its exhausts. Other engines are warming up as we drive by, and while the B Flight pilots are getting out of the lorry another one gets its run-up near by and the very earth seems to shake from the terrific power that is being unleashed.

The C.O. is in charge of A Flight (to which I belong) today, as our regular flight commander has gone on leave. He has arrived at our headquarters ahead of us and already has his flying suit on. He starts making up the schedule for our flight and writing it with chalk on the bulletin board, while we are donning our flying suits and Mae Wests (lifejackets).

In addition to its squadron markings, each airplane in a squadron had a letter painted on its side which simply designates which of the squadron's machines it is. The C.O.'s favorite machine is "D." He flies at the head of the flight, the number one machine of "Red" Section. So he writes at the top of the board:

"Red 1 — C.O. — D."

Then he looks around and says, "Percy, you like to fly 'K,' don't you?"

"Yes, sir, that's right," Percy responds.

"All right." And the C.O. writes next underneath: "Red 2 — Percy — K."

Then he turns to me. "Donny, is your machine serviceable?" He sometimes calls me "Donny" instead of my regular nickname of "Art."

"No, sir," I reply. "It's over in Maintenance today for its thirty-hour inspection. If you don't mind, I'd like to have Trevor's machine. He's off on leave. That's 'E.'"

"All right, Donny. 'E' it is, then. You can be Red 3 and Pip will be your second man, Red 4."

"If there's a squadron patrol you and Pip can do the rear guard. O.K.? That will leave the inseparables Chaddy and Jack to be Yellow One and Two. Does that sound all right to everybody?"

There are no objections. So the remaining three get their airplanes assigned, and taking our parachutes, helmets, and mittens we go out to our respective machines and get them in readiness. It's nearly eight-thirty now, and beginning to get light.

\*\*\*

Readying the Spitfire I am using, I first put my parachute on the tailplane, after making sure that there is no mist or frost where I lay it, for moisture is bad for a parachute; and I arrange its straps so that I can pick it up on the run and put it on in the shortest time. Then I hop upon the dull camouflaged wing behind the engine and climb down into the deep cockpit. There are no floor boards or upholstery or carpet, just the framework of the bottom of the fuselage to step on.

Inside the cockpit I first hang my helmet over the top of the control stick and plug in my radio cord and oxygen tube, in their places beside the seat, and make sure that the wires and oxygen tube hanging from the helmet are not twisted or tangled in any way that would interfere with my putting the helmet on quickly. I open the oxygen valves and make sure by the gauge that I have a full supply, and listen for any leaks in the connections and in the hose leading to my helmet, for a leak might cause me to run short on a long patrol.

I arrange the four seat and shoulder straps conveniently so that I can reach them and put them on quickly.

Now the all-important electric gunsight. I switch it on to make sure it's working, and check its adjustments for the range I like and the size target for which I want it adjusted. I like to have mine adjusted for Messerschmitts, thirty-two-and-one-half-foot wing span, and for a certain range. Trevor, who ordinarily uses this machine, has the sight adjusted for seventy-foot wing span, which would be a bomber, and for a longer range. I change the adjustments to suit myself and then switch it off.

Then I turn on the gasoline valves, set the throttle to the correct position for starting, set the propeller control in fully "fine" position, which will allow the engine to turn over at maximum speed for taking off, and even put the ignition switches on. I unlock the engine primer pump on the instrument panel, and flip open the cover over the starter button. Next the radiator flaps. Noting the temperature this morning, I decide that three notches closed should be about right for them, and I move the lever controlling them to that position. After I get in the air I'll readjust them to get the engine temperature right. It's bad to run the engine too hot, but worse still to run it too cold, because the guns are heated from the radiator and if the engine is running too cold they won't get enough heat and won't work!

I make sure that the pressure is up in the air system. This operates the brakes and the landing flaps on the airplane, and most important of all it is used to fire the guns. Finally I adjust the seat to its best position for me (which is the highest position, incidentally) and place my mittens in a handy place beside the throttle.

That finishes the preparations, and I climb out and return to our flight building.

These careful preparations make it possible to be off the ground in three minutes from the time we get an order to go up. Engineers and scientists and designers spend fortunes on research and strive their utmost to incorporate features in our airplanes to give us more and more speed and power with which to climb up and overtake the enemy; and each minute we can save in getting off the ground on a scramble is worth a hundred extra horsepower in trying to intercept the enemy!

In the office at our flight building I leaf through the log sheets for the various airplanes of the flight, until I find the one for the machine I'm using. In this is maintained a record of inspections, refuelings, and flights. I check to see that mechanics and armorers have signed it in the columns required, indicating that the necessary inspections have been made on airplane, engine, instruments, radio, and guns, and that it has been filled with gas and oil and cooling liquid; and then I initial it in the column headed "Pilot."

Now I can relax.

***

The building is divided into two parts: one for pilots and the other for mechanics and other ground personnel, who are all termed "troops." Through the partition between we can hear the troops laughing and chatting and playing cards and darts and "Shove Ha'penny." Their work was begun early in the morning, and most of it finished by the time we came to readiness; so now most of them have nothing to do but stand by until the machines are used.

A number of comfortable chairs are provided for us pilots to sit in around the stove, and there are also a few cots to lie on. Chaddy and Jack make for the latter, because they were on a party last night. The lights are still on, since it has just been getting daylight; but now that it's light enough two of us go around taking down the black-out blinds from the windows; and then we turn off the lights.

Percy engages Pip in a darts game, while the C.O. and I prop our feet on the stove and read the latest "Intelligence Dope" which "Number One," our Intelligence officer, left with us yesterday.

After a time, their darts game finished, Percy and Pip pull up chairs and join us around the stove where we talk fighting tactics and politics, and swap stories of our experiences. As the conversation gets interesting Chaddy and Jack get up from their cots and pull up chairs around the stove also. The C.O. tells us about his visit to the operations room at our old base last summer, just before the big blitz began, when some Spitfires of another squadron caught a German "Red Cross" plane doing reconnaissance along the English coast.

"As you know," he explains, "airplanes which carry on rescue or ambulance work have red crosses painted on them; and according to an international agreement they are not to be attacked. Of course they aren't supposed to carry out anything but rescue or ambulance work under this agreement; but you know how those Nazis are — they only recognize the parts of an agreement that work in their favor.

"They have quite a lot of ambulance planes, usually old out-of-date transport machines. Last summer it became pretty evident that they were using them for other purposes than rescue and ambulance work. They were actually flying over our own territory, getting by on our respect for this agreement not to attack them.

"However, it became so obvious that the Nazis were actually doing photography and reconnaissance work over our territory with these Red Cross machines that finally the British government informed the German government, through a neutral country, that if any more of them were found flying over our territory, under circumstances where they couldn't possibly be doing rescue work, they would be shot down.

"Well, on this morning that I was in the operations room, there was a section of three Spitfires of —— Squadron on patrol and I was sitting beside their controller, listening to their radio conversations and watching their position and that of the Hun they were looking for, as the positions were plotted about on the big map in the middle of the room. They were looking for a single enemy machine which was reported to be about, and their controller was watching their position and that of the Hun on the map, and giving them courses to steer to try to bring them together with it. We could see that they were very close to the Hun, and all at once the 'Tally-ho' went up as the boys sighted him. Then there was an intermittent conversation something like this:

"'Say, what kind of airplane is this, anyway?'

"'I don't know. Come on, let's knock it apart and see.'

"'Hold on! Wait! We can't shoot this thing, it's a rescue plane. See, it's got red crosses on it!'

"'What of it? We don't need anyone rescued over here. It's got black crosses on it too. Let's blow its head off!'"

The C.O. continues. "To make a long story short, they shot a few holes in the machine and forced it to land.

"It was a big old seaplane and landed in the water near shore and our patrol boats went out and captured it and its crew. Just as was suspected, there was no doctor on it nor even a stretcher or any kind of medical equipment. Instead, they had all sorts of cameras and photographic equipment on it. They were doing reconnaissance work and photographing our territory under the guise of rescue and ambulance work!

"It was right after that happened that the order came around to all squadrons that in the future we should shoot down any German red-cross planes found over or along our coast."

The telephone orderly comes in as our C.O. finishes the story. "Pardon, sir," he says to the C.O. "Operations are on the telephone and say there may be a 'section show' for three airplanes shortly, and they want to know which section it will be."

"Tell them it will be Red Section," our C.O. replies. Then to me: "Art, you come in with Percy and me and make the third man in the section if we go, will you? Then Pip can go into Chaddy's section and be Yellow Three if they want another section. O.K.?"

"O.K., sir," we reply.

Nothing further happens for an hour or so. I am engrossed in a newspaper story, and most of the rest are drowsing. Blond, lanky Pip is sprawled on one of the cots as only Pip knows how to sprawl, and reading a magazine.

\*\*\*

"Red Section take off!"

I come alive with a start. The telephone orderly has called it from the office, and an efficient excitement reigns.

The C.O. and Percy and I bolt for the door. Pip and Chaddy and Jack start to get up, then realize it doesn't concern them and relax again. Sergeant M—— is shouting to the mechanics, "START UP! START UP! Red Section only — D, K, and E!"

We pause going out the door just long enough to get the rest of the message from the telephone orderly.

"Patrol Chatham at ten thousand feet and watch for one bandit approaching from the southeast!" He has to shout the last, because we are already on our way to our machines. My machine is farthest away, and when I reach it I am nearly winded from running in my heavy flying clothes and boots.

Mechanics are already there, and one is in the cockpit working the primer. I grab my parachute on the run, by its top straps, swing it onto my back and snap the straps into place around me while the mechanic in the cockpit works the starter and the engine comes to life.

He climbs out, and I swing up onto the wing and squeeze into the cockpit, and with his help I fasten my seat and shoulder straps. Then on with my helmet, and I snap the oxygen mask into place across my face, fasten the chin strap, and pull up the adjusting strap at the back. Then on with my mittens, release the parking brake, and I'm taxiing out onto the field. The other two machines are taxiing out too, and I swing my machine into place to the left and rear of where the C.O. has paused with his.

I see his helmeted head turned towards Percy's machine on the other side and his mittened thumb come up. Percy's thumb comes up in reply. I already have my thumb up when he looks my way, and he turns and looks ahead and a faint puff of smoke streaks back from the exhaust of his engine; and though I can scarcely hear his engine opening up because of my padded helmet, I see his idling propeller become invisible and his machine begin to move. I open my throttle part way and feel the tremendous surge of power as my own machine begins to move. At the same time I punch a button that starts my radio receiver and another that starts a time recording attachment on the clock in my instrument panel.

The acceleration from our mighty engines is terrific, and in a few seconds our machines are skimming the ground lightly at eighty miles an hour, and now we are off and roaring up over the edge of the field. I reach down for the lever controlling the landing gear motor, disengage it from the "down" position and move it to the "up" position. The others have done likewise, and on the C.O.'s machine (which I have to watch to keep my place in formation) I can see the two landing gear "legs" to which the wheels are attached rising upward and outward, awkwardly, and disappearing into his wings. I feel two little thumps as my own wheels come up into their retracted position in the wings, where they are folded during flight to decrease wind resistance. Now I pull back my propeller pitch control lever so that the engine can run slower, and of course I keep opening and closing the throttle as needed to keep my position in relation to the C.O.

We fly in a "V" type formation. The C.O. is leading us in a steep climbing turn around the airdrome, absently turning to the left — a holdover from the days when there were air traffic rules.

I reach up with one hand and pull the transparent sliding hatch closed over my head, being careful not to get my arm out in the wind — for we are nearing two hundred miles an hour already, and at that speed the wind would throw my arm back hard enough to give it a painful jerk.

With my hatch closed it is much quieter inside. A crackling in my ears tells me that my radio has warmed up and is now working. Only a few seconds have elapsed since we left the ground, and the airdrome is already over a thousand feet below.

I hear the C.O.'s voice in my headphones, calling Control.

"Hello, Control. Hello, Control. Tiger Red One calling. Are you receiving me, please? Are you receiving me? Over."

A distant voice answers: "Hello, Tiger Red One, Tiger Red One. Control answering. Yes, receiving you loud and clear, loud and clear. Are you receiving me, please? Over."

Our C.O. replies: "Hello, Control. Tiger Red One answering. Receiving you loud and clear also. Understand you have one bandit for us, approaching Chatham from the southeast at ten thousand feet. One bandit approaching Chatham from the southeast. Have you any other information? Over."

"Hello, Tiger Red One. Yes, that is correct. No, I haven't anything new on it. Over."

"O.K., Control. Listening out."

We continue our upward climb, and during the next few minutes I check my oil pressure and radiator temperature, regulating the latter by means of my radiator flap control; adjust trimming controls so that my machine flies properly and doesn't tend to turn one way or the other or climb faster or slower than we are doing, and turn on the valve from my oxygen tank. This releases the oxygen to a regulator on my instrument panel so that, when I want to use oxygen, all I'll have to do is open another valve on the regulator. Up to ten thousand feet I won't use oxygen, saving it until we're ordered higher or are going into combat.

I turn my oxygen full on if I'm going into combat, even though that gives me a lot more than I need, because I'm sure then that there'll be no deficiency that would slow my thinking, and a surplus of it is supposed to help prevent fainting if one is wounded. This bandit we are after now must be a bomber, because enemy fighters never come over singly, and we don't consider attacking enemy bombers as "combat." It is unusual for anyone to get hurt attacking a German bomber.

In almost no time we are circling the city of Chatham, on the south side of the Thames, where the great naval dockyards are. At ten thousand feet we level off and throttle back our engines so that we are loafing at about two hundred miles an hour — which is way below the normal cruising speed of our machines, but saves gas. To the south and east is a heavy bank of clouds at about our altitude. Control calls us again:

"Hello, Tiger Red One, Tiger Red One! Steer zero-five-five and lose height to seven thousand feet. The bandit has turned and is now heading towards Southend."

We do as we are told, swinging northeast and diving slightly. We see a lot of broken clouds in that direction a little below our altitude, and guess that the bandit is taking cover in them.

Control calls again, as we are nearly over Southend: "Keep a sharp lookout. The bandit is very close to you now."

I switch on my gunsight and uncover my firing button and take it off safety. I do it absently, without the tremendous conflict of emotions that I had the first times last summer; and that is one of the very few evidences that I can see of any change that the war has made in me. I don't feel that it's hardened or toughened or aged me, but it does seem to have seasoned me to the point of nonchalance towards its savagery.

We circle about, watching for the enemy, but fail to see it. The pilot is clever, keeping himself well covered in cloud. Finally Control tells us that the bandit has turned and is heading southeast, towards Folkestone on the coast. We head in that direction, but the cloud cover in which the enemy appears to be hiding is very good, and we can't find him; though at the last we patrol well out to sea, nearly to the French coast. The bandit has apparently given up trying to bomb, and gone home.

Now we are ordered north a little way, and there, near the coast of Dover, we can see a small convoy of ships through rifts in the clouds under us. Control orders us to patrol over the convoy now, so we cruise back and forth over it at about ten thousand feet. There are broken clouds below us, and we keep track of the convoy by watching through the breaks in the clouds. Above, where we are, the sun is shining brightly. I alternately study the beautiful cloud formations as we pass over them, and watch the sky above for enemy fighters.

Our C.O. is inquisitive. "Hello, Control," he calls. "Have you any more bandits for us?"

"Hello, Tiger Red One. No, I'm sorry, there doesn't seem to be anything about at present. Business is very bad today. I will try my best to dig something up for you, though."

I switch off my gunsight and put the cover back over my firing button. We patrol our beat in the sky above the convoy for nearly an hour, during which no more bandits are reported about; and then Control orders us to land: "Sorry to have kept you up so long. I tried to find some work for you, but the Huns don't cooperate today."

We head back westward, losing height and descending through the clouds as we go, and in a few minutes have covered the sixty or seventy miles back to our airdrome and are circling preparatory to landing. Our engines are throttled well back now; and watching the C.O.'s machine I see his wheels drop from the wings and start to swing down into position for landing. I move my own landing gear control lever from the "up" position to "down"; and a few seconds later I feel thumps, and a green light comes on in my instrument panel, indicating that the wheels are down in position for landing.

I pull the sliding hatch open over my cockpit, and a rush of wind and sound greets me. I move my propeller pitch control into fully fine position, and now we are making our final gliding turn to come in to land, still in our "V" formation. I drop back and swing over to the right of the other two and take up position behind and to the right of Percy, so that we are all three in a straight line, each behind and to the right of the one in front of him, the C.O. leading. This is called "echelon" formation.

I see the C.O.'s wing flaps come down and then Percy's, and I switch the flap control on my instrument panel to the "down" position and hear a hiss of air and feel my machine surge up a little as my own landing flaps go down. These flaps cause the airplane to lose speed more quickly and to land more slowly.

We glide in over the obstructions at less than a hundred miles per hour, using our engines part of the time to help keep the machines under control at this comparatively slow speed until they are safely on the ground.

After I've taxied into place and shut off my engine I once more arrange everything "in readiness" in the cockpit, climb out and put my parachute back on the tail, and stroll back to the pilots' room with the C.O. and Percy. It was just another uneventful patrol, but we agree that it has been a pleasant ride.

When we open the door of the pilots' room Chaddy asks, "Did you see anything, sir?"

"Nope," our C.O. replies as he pulls up his chair and picks up the magazine he was reading. "We tried to find a bandit, but he couldn't make up his mind where he was going. First he approached Chatham, then Southend, then Folkestone, and he finally came to a decision on home apparently. At least we chased him nearly to France without seeing him, and he didn't come back. He was in cloud all the time, and we sort of escorted him around on his tour, it seems, without ever getting to see him. The rest of the time we spent sitting around over a convoy that's going through the Straits."

*\*\**

Once more we relax, but it's getting near one o'clock now, and soon the telephone orderly sticks his head out of the office door with the awaited message: "Operations says the squadron may now go to 'Available at call,' sir."

Our shift is over, and unless something very big starts we are off for the afternoon.

Entering the mess, I glance at the letter rack in the hall, see a letter in my box, take it out. It's from home, mailed a month ago, and I rush to my room and read it before washing up.

Having read my letter and washed, I join the rest of the boys in the dining hall. The pilots of the other squadron have had their dinner earlier because they relieved us, and most of the airdrome and Operations officers have finished eating and are in the lounge; so once again we have the dining room mainly to ourselves. Waiters bring us soup, and then we get our main course cafeteria style. There is choice of "curry and rice" or Yorkshire pudding for the main dish. Big, good-natured Sam, filling our plates, checks me. "You don't need to tell me — I know what you want when there's curry. You don't have to tell me!" And he heaps a generous helping of curry and rice on my plate. It's an English dish that I especially like, as Sam has learned long ago.

I help myself to potatoes and greens. Then we have a choice of tapioca pudding or rhubarb pie for dessert. The pie is made in a dish about the size of a dishpan, and you dip in to get what you want of it.

After lunch we may help ourselves to coffee in an urn in the hallway, in tiny cups about half the size of ordinary cups. It's atrocious compared with American coffee, though, and I seldom drink it. The only place where I've been able to get good coffee in England is the American Eagle Club on Charing Cross Road in London. (Note to Mr. Hutchinson of the Club: I expect two free cups of coffee for this plug, the next time I'm in town.)

In the lounge after lunch airdrome and Operations officers join in the conversation. Genial Squadron Leader A——, who was our controller this morning while we were on patrol, comes up to speak to our C.O. He has a pilot's wings on his uniform and three or four ribbons earned in the last war. "I'm awfully sorry I had to keep you boys up there so long this morning, but —"

"Oh, that was entirely all right," our C.O. breaks in. "We enjoyed it immensely. The weather was fine and we had a very nice ride out of it."

"Well, I'm very glad of that. There was absolutely nothing about after you chased that bandit back to France, but you know that convoy was right there passing within a few miles of the French coast, and I felt that I just had to keep some one over it. There wasn't a plane in the sky on the other side, but still if no one was on patrol and some Hun had slipped out and taken a crack at it the Navy just never would have forgiven us; and I shouldn't blame them. So I thought, as long as you boys were in the air, I'd keep you around over it for a while instead of sending out some one else."

"I'm really glad you did," our C.O. assures him. "We've hardly done any flying lately, and that sort of thing helps to keep us from getting rusty. It's a nice day, and we were just as comfortable sitting around up there as we would have been sitting around in the pilots' room on readiness; and we were a lot less bored."

I think to myself, "Is it possible that this same man we're standing beside now was the voice in our headphones that ruled us many miles away in that weird world above the clouds only an hour or so ago?"

None of us is gifted with even a fraction of the imagination we need to realize what we do when we're on patrol, what miracles we perform as part of the day's work! We were so big and fast and terrific, streaking about above the clouds out there, so completely detached from the earth, yet obeying this man's quiet distant voice; and the C.O. terms it "sitting around up there." Man's accomplishments have outstripped his capacity to comprehend them!

We spend the afternoon in various ways. We are on call, but can do anything we like as long as we stay on the airdrome. I spend some time in my room practicing on my accordion. Percy joins me with his, and we work on some pieces together. Then our C.O. brings his, and the three of us work together for a while. Percy and I are just learning, but the C.O. is a good player. The C.O. and I work on a homemade arrangement of "Carry me Back to Old Virginny" which I've worked out from the way my mother used to play it on the piano, and which the C.O. is very fond of.

After an hour's pleasant practice together we break up. The C.O. has to go to his office and take care of some work, and I have an appointment with Norman to practice on the "Link Trainer."

This is an American invention for pilots to practice blind flying — piloting by instrument. It consists of a little mock airplane mounted on a pedestal, with the closed cockpit and controls of an airplane and a complete layout of instruments. An intricate arrangement of motors and connections causes it to behave just like an airplane, and a recording attachment records on a sheet of paper the course that the student is theoretically flying.

I find Norman in the billiard room with Elby, and after they've finished their game Norman and I don our caps and Irving jackets and walk through the camp to the Link Trainer building. We take turns instructing each other in the trainer for about half an hour each. The one who is student climbs into the tiny cockpit, closes the hood so he can't see outside, and starts the motors. Then he pilots it by the instruments before him, while the one who is acting as instructor assigns the courses that he is to fly and orders him to make climbs, glides, turns, and so on, all by a little telephone arrangement.

By the time we've finished this and returned to the mess it's tea time, and we join other officers who are drifting into the dining room. Our "tea" consists of toast and marmalade or jam, two or three kinds of cake, and of course tea.

After that I wander back to my room, light the fire in my fireplace and sit down in front of this friendly little center of warmth to write a letter home: "Dear Mother and Dad: Just received your letter ..."

It's beginning to get dark, and my batman comes in and puts up the black-out blinds in front of my windows. They are wooden frameworks that fit the window frames, covered with heavy black cloth to keep any light from showing outside.

My letter finished, I wander back to the lounge, feeling restless. John and Tid are there, reading the evening papers, and I join them. It's just after six o'clock now, and the six o'clock news is being read by the B.B.C. announcer. He is saying something about an enemy bomber that "crossed the southeast coast this morning and came inland a short distance, but turned back without dropping any bombs, and returned homeward across the Channel pursued by our fighters."

A little later some one tunes the radio over to the German radio station at Bremen. The German "news" in English is being given, by the familiar pontifical voice of "Lord Haw Haw," as he is called — the Englishman who turned traitor and works for the Nazis. "This morning, bombers of the German Air Force attacked the British naval dockyards at Chatham, causing great devastation among docks and shipyards and destroying a British cruiser. They also attacked military objectives at South-end and Folkestone, wreaking terrific havoc. Immediately after this raid a British convoy attempting to pass through the Straits of Dover was attacked by our bombers, and a destroyer and six merchant ships totaling thirty thousand tons were sunk.

"A formation of twenty-five British Spitfires were guarding this convoy, but they fled at sight of our bombers. However, one of our bombers pursued them and shot down two of them. The complete destruction of the British Royal Air Force is now nearly finished; and it is definitely known that the few remaining British pilots are so exhausted and terrified that many of them refuse to take to the air when ordered to go up and intercept our airplanes."

We are only half listening, as we have been discussing whether we should go by bus down to R——, the near-by suburb of London, to take in a movie. John has just yawned and remarked: "This inaction is getting me down. I surely wish those Huns would come over and give us a scrap once in a while!"

We finally decide in favour of a movie instead of supper? and getting our overcoats and caps we leave the mess by the back door and take a short cut out of the camp to the bus stop near by. The Havana Theater is showing Bette Davis in "All This and Heaven Too," and we are soon losing ourselves in the happiness and romance and sweet sadness of this great picture.

Donald Duck snaps us out of it afterward and keeps our sides splitting with his adventures on a camping trip; and at the end we rise with the rest of the audience and stand at attention while "God Save the King" is played.

Outside after the show, we half feel our way along the darkened streets to a restaurant we know, where we have a light lunch to make up for the supper we missed.

A crowd of airmen are waiting for the bus at the stopping point when we get there, many of them from our squadron. We watch the numbers on the various busses that come down the street, until ours comes. Just two dim little lights approaching us along the dark street, and when they are close we can make out the towering outlines of the big double-decker bus, with the number "123" in dim blue light on the front, which means it's the one we want.

We swing aboard and climb the little winding stairway to the upper deck, and feel our way to seats in the gloomy interior, which is very dimly illuminated by little blue lights. Maybe two dozen airmen fill most of the seats up here, and the huge vehicle trundles off through the darkness.

As the bus sways along the lonely road the smooth whining rhythm of the motor is background and accompaniment for snatches of soldiers' ditties and ballads as some of the boys break out in song. Cockney and Irish and Yorkshire and Welsh and Scotch voices, strong and throaty, blend in songs of home and sweethearts.

Finally the bus slows down for the airdrome, and the spell is broken.

We clamber out and pass through the sentry gate after being identified, and make our way by the familiar short cut to the back door of the mess. It's misting a little, and no German planes have been over, so we guess that the weather is "closing down" and there won't be any flying tomorrow. We are only supposed to be at "fifteen minutes available" in the morning anyway, not being scheduled for readiness until afternoon; so we're pretty sure we can sleep late in the morning.

We bid one another good night, and I go to my room, take a bath, and go to bed. Another day of war, such as it is for us at this period, is over.

# CHAPTER TWELVE

# WE STAGE A COMEBACK

ONE NIGHT late in December it was specially blitzy. No bombs were dropped near us, but there were Huns droning back and forth overhead continuously for several hours. The anti-aircraft kept up an unceasing racket, and even Alfy joined the chorus more frequently than ever before, making the boys drop their ale tankards and spill their sherry in the lounge during the evening, and afterward breaking our sleep pretty frequently.

Once during the night the droning of a German machine suddenly swelled to a long agonized moaning that ceased suddenly at its very peak, and afterward we learned that it was a Junkers 88 that had been hit by antiaircraft fire and had dived into the ground nor far away.

Next morning we knew what it was all about. The great fire raid had been made on the City of London, causing England's worst fire in several centuries.

There was still no resumption in daylight activity, and during the lull we speculated a lot on its meaning. We wondered if the Huns were getting ready to start a big offensive, and most of us thought it inevitable. They had learned that on long drawn-out air offensive operations over our territory their losses were all out of proportion to their winnings in combat with us. Therefore it seemed logical to expect them to get organized for a concentrated short offensive to try to get control of the air over southeast England, the first necessary step before they can commence the one and only campaign which if successful may win them the war — the invasion of England.

The lack of German air activity in daytime seemed ominous, and we wondered when there would be a change, not knowing at first that we were to take matters into our own hands and make the first change — that we British fighter pilots, who were supposed to have been annihilated and driven from the air by the overwhelming hordes of Prussian fliers who were set upon us last summer and fall, were to show how badly we were beaten by striking the first offensive blows of the new year!

So that you will understand what a significant step it was for us to take the offensive, let me remind you of the status of the R.A.F. in the summer of 1940 when the great Battle for Britain began. Without a doubt we were greatly outnumbered. Obviously then we had to make every machine and pilot count, and could not afford the extra risks involved in fighting over the enemy's territory, where all pilots shot down would be lost because those who escaped alive would be captured, and where damaged machines that had to force-land would be lost also, together with their pilots. We could only afford to fight on our own ground, where we could keep losses to an absolute minimum. It would be a tremendous step for us to go on the offensive, significant because it would mean we had grown enough to be able to afford such risks, and doubly significant if it came now on the heels of the enemy's abandonment of such operations.

Often we longed for the time we could go on the offensive and give the Hun some of his own medicine, and wondered if it would come soon. We had been on the defensive so long that it was hard to imagine what it would be like going over enemy territory, but we grinned in anticipation of making the Nazis spend long hours "at readiness" as we did, taking off at unexpected times to go up without knowing where to expect the enemy or in what numbers.

So when the big news came shortly after the first of the year, it was like the answer to a prayer for most of us. We were to initiate things with a daylight bombing raid on a target in northwest France! A formation of bombers was to be escorted by several squadrons of Spitfires and Hurricanes, and our squadron was included.

There would be no attempt to sneak through and get away without being intercepted, for the main object of the raid was to get the Huns to come up and do battle. To add to the sting of the raid two squadrons of Hurricanes were going to "shoot up" the St. Inglevert airdromes, a cluster of airdromes that are used by the Nazis as frontline fighter bases. By this is meant they would attack with machine-gun fire, strafing personnel, gun positions, vehicles, and parked airplanes.

\*\*\*

"Zero hour" was noon one day early in January. All morning we sat around in nervous anticipation. We speculated a lot on how well prepared the Huns would be to meet us. One thing we felt sure of was that, if they intercepted us at all, it would be with an enormous mass, for we had never seen them offer to do battle without at least a three-to-one advantage in numbers.

This sounds like boasting, I realize, but it's absolutely true. Any R.A.F. fighter pilot will tell you the same, and boasting is anything but a fad in the R.A.F. On the average these boys are by far the most modest fellows I've known, and I've knocked about quite a lot. The average of them has less to say about the time he faced a dozen Messerschmitts alone (as most of them have) and came back with half his tail and an aileron shot away, than the average American commercial pilot whom you can hear around any big city airport telling about the time he flew clear across Lake Deepwater with a spark-plug wire on one of his nine cylinders getting looser and looser.

One of "B" Flight's pilots, a very young-looking fair-haired kid whom we called "Toss," was particularly excited. He sat or stood around all morning, grinning from ear to ear in anticipation, and saying: "We're for it. We're for it now! We'll have a party for sure this time!"

We took off for our rendezvous at the appointed place and time. Circling slowly we fell into our prearranged position with the other squadrons of fighters and the bombers, and in a few minutes we were sweeping down across the Thames

Estuary, cutting southeast over Kent, across the cliffs near Dover, and out over the Channel. We must have been a formidable sight to the German observers on the coast of France as we approached, for as far as I know this was the biggest British formation that had ever flown in war. There were over a hundred machines — not nearly as many as the Nazis had used in their big raids on England last summer, not as many as my squadron had often faced alone; but we made a pretty good-sized cloud just the same, and it was certainly more than the Nazis had ever had to face before!

We were to enter France from the north, between Calais and Dunkirk where the coast runs almost east and west. We flew eastward almost parallel with the coast until we were about by Calais, then started swinging in. I had had trouble with my fingers getting cold on the way, but now that we were nearing France I found that they weren't bothering any more. My circulation had speeded up enough!

As we started coming in over the coast black puffs of smoke began unfolding here and there in the air about us, as if by magic. The Germans have very heavy concentrations of anti-aircraft batteries along the coast, and they were going full swing. By the time we crossed the coast the air about us was well peppered. None of their shots came close enough though, so we didn't have to change course. This was reassuring, and I began to feel more at ease.

Now that we were crossing into a foreign country, I had an impish desire to call out on the R/T and ask the boys if they all had their passports ready. I would have, if we hadn't been told not to "do any natting over the R/T" until the raid was over.

The two squadrons of Hurricanes that were to attack the St. Inglevert airdromes detached themselves from the formation about the time we entered France, and went down. They would do their attack at very low altitude. All of us were scanning the sky closely now, watching for the expected horde of Huns who we felt would be coming to intercept us.

I began to speculate on the confusion at the Nazi airdromes, when for the first time in the war they were getting a real alarm. I imagined Nazi pilots having to rush out from dinner, from bed, from the bar, and from wherever else they might be — the confusion of getting transportation to their drome, and all the other difficulties incidental to an unexpected call to arms. "Hurry, we're being invaded!" "Where's my helmet?" "Where's Hans?" "Run and get Wolfgang out of bed — if he's sober!" I almost forgot my business of watching for them in my speculations on what excitement our appearance must have caused among them. It made me feel good. They were getting some of their own at last!

We kept swinging around in a gentle right-hand turn, first to the south, then southwest, then west, so that finally we were headed home again, although we were now well inside France. Still we could see no signs of enemy planes.

The bombers were passing over their target now, and I began to think they hadn't dropped their bombs yet, for there was no sign of any smoke in the target area. Suddenly a series of volcanic explosions began occurring all about in the target area, with debris flying up and great clouds of smoke following. They had dropped their bombs all right, but I'd forgotten it would take a little time for the bombs to get down to the ground. It looked to me as if they'd covered the area pretty thoroughly, and very accurately.

We passed a little south of the St. Inglevert airdromes, the ones that the Hurricanes were "shooting up," and I grinned at the unforgettable sight there. The twenty-four Hurricanes were making themselves look like a hundred, all milling about over the airdromes in a mass of wheeling, diving, zooming, twisting and turning machines, as each pilot dived down to machine-gun a target and then zoomed up to turn and dive back in again. It was like a bunch of bees swarming. Most of these pilots were Canadians ("Crazy Canadians," our C.O. jokingly termed them in warning us all to stay clear of them while they were on this job), and they were surely acting the part now. I wondered what would happen to any unhappy Messerschmitt that would have the misfortune to blunder into their midst! The Canadians were exhausting the accumulated steam from many weeks of virtual idleness in this attack, and making a job of it.

Now the bombers, whom we were trailing, were approaching the coast, and the air beneath them became full of the angry black puffs of smoke from anti-aircraft shells sent up by the coastal guns again. We were passing out near Cape Gris Nez, where I fought my first air battle last summer. By the time we reached the coast the antiaircraft smoke was like a long black cloud just beneath us, with flashes from fresh explosions agitating about in it. All of the fire was too low to bother us, and most of it seemed to be erratic in direction also. Only once or twice I felt little jolts in the air from shells that exploded somewhere beneath us.

Then we were out over the Channel again, and I realized that the raid was over and we hadn't seen a single enemy airplane. We had singed Hitler's mustache and given Herr Goring a nice little punch in his fat middle, and were getting away without even a fight! Big in its significance, the raid, as far as we were concerned, might just as well have been a little cross-country practice trip. Not one of us had fired his guns, and none of us had been fired at, except by the anti-aircraft guns which practically don't count.

It was while we were crossing the Channel on the way home that the only fighting took place, though we didn't know about even this until afterward. It appeared that three Messerschmitts followed us out over the Channel — keeping a safe distance behind and trying to look brave, thinking it was all over, I suppose. They probably planned to tell their superiors how they had routed us and chased us home. But of course they didn't know about the Hurricanes that were still behind us, making sure that everything worth while that they could find on the St. Inglevert airdromes was riddled. These Hurricanes finally got through and followed us a few minutes later, just in time to come across the three unhappy Messerschmitts, and they shot all three down into the sea.

It was a nice little trip, and it boosted our morale a lot. The papers made a big thing of it, and every one in London was talking about it for the next few days. It made people feel good to know that we were giving the Nazis some of their own, and it boosted their confidence by proving that the R.A.F. was so far from being annihilated by the German blitz that it could administer blows of its own.

Don't confuse this with the night raiding and bombing, which is always carried out by both sides when weather permits, under cover of darkness when the chance of combat is negligible; nor with small daylight bombing raids using cloud cover. Those two kinds of bombing have always been carried on by both sides. It's the raids in broad daylight, where the enemy has a chance to see the raiders and do battle to stop them, that the Nazis ceased last fall and we began with this raid in January.

The weather turned foggy the next day, and at noon our squadron was released for the rest of the day. Tommy, my new flight commander, and I wanted to see the fire damage in the City of London; so we went downtown and spent the afternoon there.

The City of London is a borough in the central part of London that contains the buildings of many large banking and business firms. The section that was burned out was roped off, but we managed to get in on the strength of our uniforms. It was a ghastly sight — silent streets lined with empty stone skeletons of once magnificent buildings, the fire-blackened walls still standing with blank windows and nothing inside but heaps of brick and rubble. All about was the haunting smell of burned wood. We were shown through the ruins of the Guildhall, London's once magnificent city hall, scene of countless historical events; and told the official who showed us through it that each of us would remember this the next time he got a Hun in his sights. There was no possible military objective anywhere in the vicinity, and it was truly an "act of vandalism by the greatest vandal of all time."

One scene I don't think I'll ever forget, as an example of the indestructibility of the British spirit. Near the outskirts of the area which was burned out we followed a street on one side of which all the buildings were burned. Most of the buildings on the other side were burned out, too; but sandwiched in between two large buildings that were completely burned out so that only the walls stood, we saw a little ladies' dress shop that had somehow been saved. The walls outside were black from the fire; the windows, cracked, and the window frames, scorched. Bricks and rubble blocked the street in front of it.

But the sidewalk was swept clean, and that little shop, with ghastly fire-blackened desolation all around it, burned-out stone buildings towering around it on both sides of the narrow street — that little shop was still open for business, and doing business, with its windows filled with a neat display of ladies' dainty underthings!

\*\*\*

Weather of course interfered a great deal with the operations of both sides through the winter, but the R.A.F. let few opportunities pass to follow up their initial daylight air offensive. Practically every day of good weather R.A.F. fighter squadrons made sweeps over France, sometimes escorting more bombing raids and sometimes just going by themselves, but always giving the Nazis a chance to do battle if they would.

Our squadron wasn't always on these sweeps, or raids, for the work was rotated among a number of squadrons; and I didn't necessarily go each time our squadron went, because we now had plenty of spare pilots and the work was rotated among us. There's little formality about the distribution of flying duties in an average R.A.F. fighter squadron. The spirit of the boys is such that all want to do their share, and it's run like a big family, with the C.O. permitting the boys to work out their own schedules usually, subject to his approval.

When there is a 100 per cent reserve of pilots in the squadron, usually about a third are away at any one time, either on leave or on forty-eight-hour passes; and for the most part the pilots arrange among themselves who is to work on what days, who is to go on leave when, etc., making a schedule that will be most suitable to all while allowing for an equal distribution of work.

Our squadron went on a number of raids and sweeps during January and February, over Belgium as well as France, and even parts of Holland. Never on these sorties did any of us get a chance to use his guns. The same was true of most of the rest of the squadrons. Occasionally a few Huns would approach our formations at high altitude and watch for a chance to drop on a straggler, but there was never a sign of any real attempt to do battle. Nor did they make any offensive sweeps of their own until late in February, when they began sending a formation over very high once in a while, to scurry home as soon as our fighters reached their altitude and they saw they would have to fight if they stayed any longer.

Thus the winter went on, while we pilots flew a little and loafed a lot, always wondering when the big blitz would start again.

One foggy morning a section of three of our machines was sent out over the North Sea after a bandit. They were Jimmy leading the section, Toss, and John. John came back ahead of the rest, and when he taxied up it was easy to see why. His guns had been fired, his bulletproof windscreen was badly mangled, and there were big holes in his wing and fuselage.

They had intercepted a Junkers 88 bomber (a larger type than the Junkers 87 dive bomber), and its rear gunner had done this to John's machine with cannon fire. The other two boys soon came in, to say they had both fired on the Junkers but finally lost it in the clouds. They thought it was going down but of course couldn't claim a victory. However, a few hours later they got confirmation. An SOS from the crew had been intercepted, stating that they had crashed in the sea and abandoned the airplane and were floating in their life raft.

A little later a German ambulance airplane flew to the spot and picked them up, the R.A.F. making no attempt to interfere. So that established the victory, and it was awarded to the boys as confirmed — one — third to each pilot. It was the first engagement any of us had had in the new year.

# CHAPTER THIRTEEN

# INTERLUDE

EARLY IN THE WINTER our C.O. had told me he was trying to get me an opportunity to go home on leave; and quietly through the winter he had been working on it. Even when prospects began to look good I couldn't believe it, and I said little about it in my letters home except that I had an application in. Somehow it didn't seem possible that I could leave while this war of which I was part was still going on, and actually live again in the old kind of world with no enemies and no black-outs and no bombing nor readiness periods nor patrols, and with good coffee and cars running on the right side of the street. I said I wouldn't believe it until I was on the boat!

Late in February an order came transferring me to a new squadron. I hated to leave the old bunch whom I knew so well; the order had come with little warning, and I had to leave right away; so I avoided farewells as much as possible and got off.

My new squadron mates were fine fellows like all the rest of the R.A.F. They took me on a party the first night I was with them, and in twenty-four hours I was feeling right at home.

Their work was a little different, and there has been some publicity about their, or rather our, activities. However, I won't go into that now. They used the same type Supermarine Spitfires that my old squadron had, and I got along all right.

Only a few days later a message came through to the squadron's headquarters: "Pilot Officer Donahue report to Embarkation Officer at —— not later than ——." I knew what it meant: my trip to America, which had been only a dream, was to become a reality!

The message gave me three days' notice, and during the next two I spent my spare time packing the things I wanted to take, making last-minute preparations, and pinching myself to prove that I was awake and it was really happening. I was to leave on the noon train, and the last day I did the early morning patrol with Tony, my flight commander.

As I took off on what was to be my last flight in an indefinite time I uttered a little prayer that I might finally find a Hun. I still hadn't used my guns since the engagement on Armistice Day!

We cruised across the Channel into France in hope of "scaring something up," and I watched the sunrise from above clouds over Dunkirk at twenty-five thousand feet. We hadn't found a sign of life in the air when Control called us and warned us that "you're getting your feet pretty wet" — which sounded like a hint that he'd feel better if we were closer home.

So we headed back. As we neared the English coast, Control told us a bandit was approaching us from the south at about eight thousand feet. There was a heavy bank of clouds at that height, so we knew the bandit must be approaching in them. They ended about five miles south of us, so that if he kept coming our way he would shortly break out into clear air where we could see him and perhaps intercept him. It undoubtedly was a bomber trying to get to England without being seen.

We approached the edge of the clouds, and Control said, "The bandit is very close to you now."

I switched on my gunsight and turned my firing button off safety, watching the edge of the clouds closely and fervently hoping that my prayer would be answered and a bomber would make its appearance; but minutes went by, and no Hun appeared. Then Control called and told us the bandit had gone back towards France. Hearing new voices over the R/T, I knew that it was the next patrol coming up to relieve us, telling Control that they were in the air. Then Control called us and told us we might land; and regretfully I took a last look at France and switched off my gunsight and put my firing button back on safety and turned back to our base.

At the last minute before I left the airdrome for the train I remembered promising to bring home some pieces of a German plane for souvenirs; so I hunted and found some pieces of a Messerschmitt dumped behind one of the buildings, tore off a few strips of metal wing-covering, and packed them in my things.

The voyage was rough and seemed endless. I am a poor sailor, and though I managed to eat my meals pretty regularly I found that there were a bunch of rules which my stomach dictated for me: principally that I couldn't concentrate my gaze on one thing while the ship was rolling; and that prevented my reading. No radios can be used on ship either, for it is found that ships can be located by radio impulses that radio receivers themselves send out sometimes.

We were cut off from the world except for daily news summaries which were received on the ship's wireless and typed out and posted in the passengers' lounge; and for the sight of the other ships in the convoy. I would stand out on deck by the hour watching the waves and the other ships and trying to read the signals flashed back and forth between the ships by means of signal lamps.

One Sunday forenoon the weather was absolutely lousy. It alternately rained and snowed and sleeted. Waves broke over the front of the ship as it heaved and tossed, and nearly drenched those of us who were on deck. Visibility was very low, and we could scarcely see the other ships in the convoy.

We passengers were never informed of our position; but we had been sailing so long that we didn't see how we could help being nearly "there." Also some unusual activities of the crew suggested that something was afoot. Looking off to our port I saw what looked like a low dark cloud nearly hidden by the mist, and I watched it for several minutes, until I knew it couldn't be a cloud, because it had trees on it!

***

This is supposed to be a story of war, so I'll go lightly over this interlude of peace. I was to have about a week at home, and I planned to spend it getting in some good exercise on my father's farm, to make up for some of the loafing I'd done through the winter.

I didn't get in much work. A crowd met me at the train in my home town, and I found myself almost a celebrity! I had more invitations than I could possibly accept to speak at various gatherings and over the radio. The Commercial Club of St. Charles gave a banquet in my honor and presented me with a wonderful gold wrist watch and my mother with a bouquet of flowers. The Kiwanis of Minneapolis gave me a silver loving cup. Friends were coming to see me all the time, and I was deluged with letters — even to receiving fan mail! Most of the week I was in a daze, every one was so good to me.

The lights at night were as strange to get used to as the black-out had been when I first went to England. Especially when I was inside a brightly lighted place at night and opened the door to go out, absently expecting to see nothing but darkened streets and houses and little dim lights on cars, I would be bewildered for a moment by the bright street lights, neon signs, and blinding headlights of cars flashing by!

It was also strange being in civilian clothes again, for I was unable to wear my uniform: according to international law I must be interned for appearing in the uniform of a belligerent nation. It was strange too, to see so many young men in civilian clothes, and no British uniforms — and to walk down the street without having to reply to salutes continually. The few uniforms I did see looked very odd, after being used to seeing British and allied uniforms for so long.

I found it hard to realize the change in popular opinion that had taken place in the United States in the few months I was gone, and the widespread awakening to the peril which the many-phased Nazi march of conquest holds for America; though in the papers I occasionally saw strange manifestations of it.

A pilot officer in the Royal Air Force, such as myself, earns the equivalent of about $88.00 per month, out of which he must pay for his meals, keep up his uniform, and pay about $6.00 per month income tax. It was hard to believe that, among a people ninety per cent convinced that their safety depends on England's victory, factory workers engaged in industries vital to that victory were striking and delaying production and jeopardizing England's chances.

The average American aircraft factory worker certainly earns more than the British pilots flying the aircraft he builds, and works much shorter hours. Yet I read of their striking for still more pay, though every day of strike by workers in aircraft factories means that boys who are fighting their battles will die for the want of the new equipment. The more airplanes and guns and tanks America can furnish England now, the fewer she may have to produce for herself and man with her own sons later, for England can be depended on to use them to the greatest advantage against the common enemy.

If Germany wins this war there will be no "American standard of living" such as we have known. America will be forced to impoverish herself and her people in the greatest armament race in history to forestall the inevitable Nazi encroachment in the Western Hemisphere; and in that program there will be no room for maintenance of the old living standards against the Nazis' advantage of slave labor from defeated countries. It seemed foolish for Americans to be using methods to raise their standard of living which jeopardize their very existence as Americans — standard of living and all!

I did manage to spend a little time working on my father's farm, and it was strange to be doing the familiar tasks I knew so well on the farm just as if nothing had ever happened, while in my pocketbook I carried a little piece of pasteboard that read:

*Return Ticket*
*Southern Railway*
*LONDON*
*(Charing Cross)*
*to*
*F——*

# CHAPTER FOURTEEN

# THE WATCH OVER THE CHANNEL

I ARRIVED BACK in London early in the morning of the 17th of April. The sky was cloudless, like the morning in July when I first saw London. In other ways it was a painful though dramatic contrast.

On that other morning the city had been peaceful except for preparations for what was to come, and the air was fresh and clear.

This was the morning after the greatest bombardment that London had received, and the sun was a red ball glowing feebly through the haze of brown smoke that covered the city. Fire fighters were working everywhere; streets were roped off, littered with broken glass and scattered brick and masonry and other rubble; fire hoses lay all about. Piles of rubble marked where buildings had stood the day before.

Other buildings still stood, burned out or burning out inside. Here and there was a great pit in the middle of a street, with dirt and rock scattered all about and water from broken mains flooding the street. Firemen were still working heroically against the flames of buildings struck by fire bombs; and A.R.P. workers toiled in the debris of buildings hit by high-explosive bombs, to rescue persons trapped inside.

The London firemen are my heroes there. The risk they take in fighting fires during air raids is terrible, for the whole scheme of Nazi bombing is to have the first planes of the raid loaded with fire bombs and manned by the best crews, who locate the targets and set them on fire, so that the machines that follow with the high-explosive bombs have only to aim at the fires.

The firemen attack these fires unflinchingly, knowing that the fires they are fighting are targets for more bombs. Their casualties are very high and their work exhausting, but nothing seems to stop them.

I remember particularly one rather youngish man, in the uniform of the Auxiliary Fire Service, drinking a cup of tea as he leaned against a mobile canteen that was stopped close to the burning building that he was working on. It was nearly noon, and he had obviously been up all night. His uniform was drenched, torn, and plastered with mud from brick and cement dust. His blond hair was matted and tousled under his steel helmet. His face was grimy and smoke-stained, and his nose bloodied, and he seemed a little groggy; but he was grinning just the same. Like a boxer standing back in a neutral corner, along about the twelfth round.

Waiting for the train that would take me to my squadron, I entered the crowded restaurant at the station and sat down for tea. A lady sat down at the same table, looking tired and a little stunned. She told me that she lived just outside London, but had a little restaurant in town. She had spent the day winding up her business as best she could, because her place had been blasted to bits the night before. And she was only one of many. Those Americans who would rather wait and have war come to them, than let their sons fight abroad, could take a lesson from that and many things much worse that I saw that day.

The trainman at the gate looked a little curiously at the crumpled and battered return ticket that I showed him. It was nearly two months since I had used the first half of it.

It was swell to get back to the squadron, though I felt a little bit like a prodigal after being away so long. The boys were all tickled to see me and to get the cigarettes and other things I had brought from America. They were throwing a party in the mess that night, so that I couldn't have arrived at a better time.

I was glad to learn that they had had some very successful operations while I was gone. "Killer" McKay, as the newspapers call him, had added a bar to his Distinguished Flying Medal, having got his twelfth confirmed victory. Two of the boys had been badly wounded though, and at least one of them, Sergeant Mann, is not expected to be able to fly again. He was awarded the Distinguished Flying Medal while in the hospital.

This boy had been shot down for the sixth time. His machine was badly shot up and his engine wrecked over the Channel, but he managed to glide back over land. Then when he was only about two hundred feet up, too low to bail out, his machine caught fire and he had to force-land it in a farmer's field. He crawled out of the cockpit then, and in spite of the fact that he was terribly burned, he took his camera out of his pocket, carefully adjusted it for light and distance, and snapped two pictures of the blazing wreck, after which he staggered across two fields to the farmhouse!

As you may recall, this is not my original squadron. I was posted to it a few days before I went to America. Naturally I wanted to get in touch with my former squadron and find out how they were; and I did so, by telephone, the first night.

The news I got didn't help me to sleep well that night, and clouded my otherwise joyous return to action. If there had been heavy fighting while I was gone, as in the blitz of August and September, 1940, I should have known that I couldn't expect the boys to be all right. But I knew the fighting had been slight, with both British and German casualties comparatively minor, and I had high hopes that my old bunch would be unchanged. The news I got was hard to take.

Pip and Norman are both gone. John is missing, but there is a possibility that he is alive, a prisoner of war. I hope so.

Nearly as hard to take as the deaths of Pip and Norman was the news that the C.O., whom we idolized and who had done so much for me, including making my trip to America possible, is a prisoner of war. That news was a source of joy to the boys when it came, because they had seen him shot down over France under circumstances that seemed to make it impossible for him to get out alive, and they had sadly given him up for dead.

We hope that he will be treated well, and from what we hear of the treatment the Germans accord their prisoners he probably will. According to an international agreement they are required to give their prisoners the same food and pay as they give the equivalent ranks in their own forces. This is checked up on by the Red Cross.

Just before I went to America on leave, Gillies and I were patrolling at low altitude one morning when we sighted a set of fifteen vapor trails high up, coming across from France. As we were too low and too few to do anything about it we just watched them and, when they were nearly to the English coast, saw one turn around and go back, apparently with engine trouble. They were Messerschmitt 109's on offensive patrol.

When they got over England we were right under them, and three of them came down towards us; we thought we were going to have a fight, but they went away again. It was an insignificant occurrence, and I thought no more about it.

Then a day or two after I got back from leave, Gillies showed me a picture from The Aeroplane of a formation of German planes making vapor trails, and I recognized it as the formation we had seen, including the one which turned back!

I'm sorry I can't tell much about the work of my present squadron, because it's very interesting. However, it is different from that of other fighter squadrons, and to a certain extent secret. I'll quote from what one London newspaper was permitted to say about us recently. This is from a write-up in *The People*, headed "Britain's Cavalry of the Air":

*Air Station, South-East England, Saturday*
*The Spitfire pilots at this station think nothing of a little before-breakfast "singeing of Hitler's moustache" raid. They are a kind of cavalry of the air, scouting in front of the main forces and operating almost entirely over the Channel or enemy territory.*

*These young pilots, spearhead of our attack — their work is mostly offensive — have a different job to the rest of the R.A.F.*

*Our bombers may go out on specific jobs, our fighters on interceptions. But these Channel patrols are up harrying, probing, prying, making lightning machine-gun raids and generally being a nuisance.*

*When they go off on a routine "reco" — reconnaissance flight — they never quite know what they will find. They are liable to drop in for a lot of unlooked-for trouble, and generally come out of it very well ...*

\*\*\*

The whitecapped waves of the French coastal waters were rocketing backwards a few hundred feet below us, and just over our heads, five hundred feet above the sea, scattered fluffy clouds were billowing past. Heavier clouds obscured the sun. It was very early on a dull murky morning a few days after my return from America, and Tony (my flight commander) and I were doing the dawn patrol. We were flying low over the sea about three or four miles north of the French coast near Calais, heading westward for home after having been out near Dunkirk. What we had been doing there will have to be left untold, but my thoughts were mainly on whether the cooks would be up yet in the mess when we got home, so that we could get breakfast, and was wishing it was possible to get something to eat early on mornings when we did the dawn patrol.

Control had just warned us over the R/T that there were six or more bandits near us, but it didn't worry us much. He is always anxious when we're in enemy territory, and frets a lot over nothing. We are ever on the alert against surprises, and if we ran into too many Huns we'd just pull up and lose them in the broken clouds close above us. I didn't even turn on my gunsight or take the firing button off its safety position. I can do that in a second nowadays.

We flew abreast of each other, wide apart, so that we could watch each other's tail. I took a few seconds to check my engine instruments and fuel supply, and when I looked back again I got a little jolt.

Two Messerschmitt 109's were streaking along just above the water a few hundred yards behind us, coming up for a surprise attack! They were camouflaged dark, with their noses painted yellow. Behind them were six more in close formation.

I called out over the R/T "Bandits astern," and waited just long enough to see Tony zoom upwards towards the clouds, indicating that he'd heard me. Then I too zoomed up, switching my gunsight on and my firing button to the "FIRE" position. I still didn't know if there was going to be a fight.

The clouds were so scattered that they gave scant cover, and I pulled on up above them and turned one way and then the other to keep anything from getting on my tail. A moment later the pair who had been closest behind us popped up through the clouds ahead of me, which meant that they had overshot me because of the turns I was doing, and the fight was on!

I took a snap shot at long range at one of them, and it was swell to hear the bedlam again and smell the powder smoke and feel a Spitfire shudder and slow from the recoil as the guns roared. Then I let him alone and took after the other, which had swung across in front of me. I chased him about among the clouds for a wild minute or so, shooting at every chance, as he twisted and ducked about trying to lose me. Twice I saw small pieces fly back off his machine as I was firing, and I finally lost him in the clouds.

Zooming up above the clouds again I saw three or four others near me, and maneuvering about violently to keep any of them from getting on my tail, I got a short "beam" shot at one as he crossed in front of me and then took after another and chased him a little way and got a short shot at him just before I lost him in the clouds.

For a moment I found myself alone, but then another popped up through the clouds in front of me, coming straight towards me head on. He was about fifty feet below my level and about three hundred yards in front, and if he pulled up his nose a little he could shoot at me. But he made no attempt to do so — just flew straight ahead, while I lost no time in nosing down until my sights centered on him and letting him have it until I had to break off to avoid a collision. I started to turn around to follow him after we'd passed, and saw when I looked back that he was no longer flying straight and level but was going down in about a forty-five-degree dive, with black smoke rippling back from under his fuselage. The realization of what I'd done awed me a little. I swung on around as he disappeared through a very thin cloud and followed him right down under the cloud but wasn't in time to see him crash. There was no sign of him. Then I stooged around under the clouds for a minute, hoping to see some signs of wreckage in the sea. I was sure he had crashed, for he was so low when I last saw him that he couldn't have straightened out before hitting the sea. Even if he had I should have seen him in the air above the sea.

Then a formation of six came along low over the water, probably the same six that had been behind the two who first tried to attack us, and I decided there were too many people here and pulled into some heavy clouds. When I last saw them they had made no move to follow me, and they may not have seen me.

I had a little difficulty in the clouds then. My compasses were spinning like tops, and my "artificial horizon," which is the main instrument used in blind flying, leered at me from where it lay, almost upside down over in one corner of its cage. It always goes haywire in a dog fight and takes a while to start working again. Finally my "directional gyro" compass quieted down so that I could hold a straight course by it, though it wouldn't tell me what course it was until I checked it by the magnetic compass; but by flying straight and level for a while I got my magnetic compass to steady down also — and found that I was steering in the direction of Holland.

When finally I got turned around and headed for home, I broke out of the clouds and didn't need the instruments any more anyway.

All this time I had practically forgotten about Tony, not having seen him. In a dog fight it's every one for himself, and each pilot is too busy to think about any one else. Now I anxiously called to him over the R/T, asking if he was all right. My radio wasn't tuned right, and I didn't understand his reply; but it was a relief to hear him anyway. I answered back, "I cannot understand your message, but your voice sounds very good!"

On the ground we got each other's stories, and I found that I'd given him some anxiety. He had heard my warning at the start, and had pulled up through the clouds just as I had, turning about to avoid being attacked from behind. But he must have turned in a different direction, for he saw no more Huns; nor did he see me. After a moment he went back down under the clouds but couldn't see any signs of life there either, and he began calling me to find out where I was. I must have had my receiver tuned very badly, or have been just too intent on my work to hear — perhaps a little of both; anyway I never heard him, and when I didn't reply after several calls he asked Control to try to get me.

Control called me several times without getting any answer, and Tony began searching the sea for me, presuming that I was shot down and reflecting how heroically I had warned him of the danger with my last words! Tony said that Control finally called him and told him in the most doleful tones, "I am afraid that I can get no reply from him."

And then a minute later he heard me calling him, and it was like a voice from the dead!

When he learned that all the time he was so worried about me I was having the time of my life in a swell dog fight that he had missed out on completely, he was more than disgusted.

I was hoping to be credited with a confirmed victory on the strength of having seen the 109 going down so obviously finished, but couldn't say I'd actually seen it crash, so that I was only credited with a "probable." If it had been near our own coast I'd have been all right, for then observers on the coast would probably have seen it crash. Later we learned that radio messages had been picked up from the squadron leader of the German formation at the time, calling one pilot for several minutes, and then asking all the other pilots in the formation if they had seen him; and all of them answered that they hadn't. So, although I could only count it as a "probable" I felt that it was at least a "very probable"! I was also credited with a "damaged" in addition, on the strength of having seen pieces flying off the second plane that I fired at; so it wasn't such a bad job of work to get done all before breakfast anyway!

\*\*\*

That just about brings the story up to date. It's the best account I can give of my war experiences, subject to the restrictions of censorship, and I hope it has been half as interesting for you to read as it has been for me to live it!

Perhaps I should wind it up by touching on the emotional side; I've thought of it. But it might look melodramatic, and I think I'll just leave that.

I'm writing in our pilots' room, wearing my Mae West and flying boots. It's a clear sunny afternoon in May, and Gillies and Perkins and I have just had a pleasant walk along a winding, shaded country road, lined with bluebells and violets. Somewhere overhead we could hear the distant moaning of Messerschmitt 109's on offensive patrol, but the other flight was on duty then and so we thought nothing of them. It's Saturday, and we met some little school kids out on a tramp, all six to eight years of age. They paid no attention to the Messerschmitts either, smiled at us shyly and impishly as we passed them, and went on chattering after we were gone.

I can hear some 109's overhead now, and I know that somewhere up there, trying to locate them, is the patrol which Chris and I shall be relieving in another half-hour.

If I step outside the door and look southeast I can see the French coast all the way from Dunkirk down to Boulogne, resting along the farther edge of the clear blue expanse of water which bounds the no man's land of the air war.

In the great deep blue sea of air above this water, eerie and scary, the watch over the Channel carries on.